DAMN! WHY DID I WRITE THIS BOOK?

by

JTG

Co-Authored by Thomika Paul

Edited by Ryan Nemeth

CONTENTS

Disclaimer

Forward

A Childhood Dream

Heat

Mr. Big Shot

Ohio Valley Wrestling

Do You Know How to Fu@ing Read?*

Hired...

...and Almost Fired

10 Matches in a Row

The Heart Breaker

The Window Seat

The Mule

Beauty Salon

Wrestler's Court

The Day Cryme Stopped

Comeback

Shade on the Shades

Fines, Fines, Yeah, Yeah

The B Word

Choose Your Words Wisely

Jim Henson

JTG, Can I Talk to You?

My First Signs

The Massage

The Tweets Heard 'Round the World

The Headphones

My Last Match

The Finisher

Q & A

The Heat Commandments

Wrestling Slang for Dummies

Acknowledgments

DISCLAIMER

Damn! Why Did I Write This Book? is intended for entertainment purposes only. Every story in this book is written from the point of view of the author, and is based on his perception of the events depicted. This book is not by any means an attempt to defame the character or persona or any person, persons, company, or companies mentioned or referred to. Any names, stories, or likenesses within the pages of this book are, again, intended to entertain the reader. And while the stories in this book are not fictional, they are, however, one-sided. Please read with that in mind.
So, save your lawsuits!

FORWARD

A forward is a short piece of writing placed at the beginning of a book, used to introduce the author and the topic. Often the Forward is typically written by a more accomplished and successful author, or an expert in the topic at hand, if you will. An opening statement by an eminent and well-respected expert gives the book added credibility. It helps the author; in a way, it's a stamp of approval on the book. So, in classic JTG fashion (and in an attempt to increase the number of people I've already pissed off, thereby bathing in the heat I've become so comfortable in) I'm writing my own shit!

JTG is *the* flyest mothafucka out of Brooklyn, NY. He's a smart, handsome, and incredibly sexy man. He should have been a 5-time World Heavyweight Champion, but as we all know, wrestling (like everything else) is controlled by politics. This book, in my (not so) humble opinion, will be a ground-breaking, earth-shattering experience for readers from all walks of life. If you ask me, it should receive a Nobel Prize in Literature. If this literary masterpiece, that will undoubtedly change countless lives, does not make The New York Times Best-Seller List within a week, well, what can I say: politics.

I will conclude by simply stating: I guarantee you will enjoy this fine piece of literature, and I guarantee that you will be moved to the point of tears by the plethora of struggles that I overcame. (Additionally: if you are one of the many people from my past who happens to read this book see a *familiar* story, and you don't like what I said about you: Oh, well. F@#K IT!)

A CHILDHOOD DREAM

People dream their entire lives of becoming a WWE Superstar. I vividly remember my five year-old self, in the living room of my Brooklyn apartment, jumping off of the arm of the couch, high above my sister's cabbage patch doll that lay on the hardwood floor. I was mimicking WWF Superstar "Macho Man" Randy Savage. *"Ooooh Yeah!"* Like most kids that love wrestling, I vowed right then and there that when I grew up, I would be a professional wrestler. Unlike most kids however, I didn't give up. This wasn't some wild fantasy that I would later toss to the side and chalk up as the wild imagination of a preschool mind; I was going to be a wrestler no matter what. It was a dream that I held tight to throughout my childhood and teenage years. I nurtured this dream. Once I graduated from high school I knew that I would not be headed off to college like most of my friends. And I wasn't going to follow in the foot steps of my sister and cousins and join the military. However uncertain the road may be, I was going to be a WWE Superstar. I wanted to make sure that some other five year-old, in some other living room, would jump off some other couch- only this kid wouldn't be idolizing Macho Man. He would be idolizing *me*.

Chea!

Fast forward to adulthood.

Hopeful men and women train for many years to make it to the "big time." It's an unthinkable life journey to most people. You sacrifice time with family and friends. You push your body to the limit. You work odd, low-paying jobs. You save money by eating cheap tuna and ramen three times a day. You do all this, you make all these sacrifices, in the hope that one day you can sit down and eat surf & turf with your new best-buddy, The Undertaker. Those kind of thoughts- enjoying the fruits of your labor and wining and dining with your childhood hero, are sometimes the only things that keep you going. You train hard in the ring, you hit the gym twice a day, and you *go go go*, and we do *not* stop until you get there. Eventually you get noticed, because you, my friend, have charisma. You get a try-out match, and you blow their socks off.

Then suddenly, *Hallelujah Sweet Baby Jesus*, you hear the magic words you've been dreaming of: "Hey Kid, how would you like a contact with the WWE?"

Hell Yeah! You don't even read it. You just sign on the dotted line.

So, you've signed your contract, get called up to the road, and guess what? Vince has big plans for you! You make your television debut! It's smooth sailing from there, right? After all, you've trained for this and dreamed of this your entire life. The writers are even sending you emails, asking you for your opinions. That's right- the writers want to know what *you* think! This is unbelievable!

Wow! You matter! You're a star! And the best part- the best part of all- is that the crowd loves you. They LOVE you. They're screaming your name in Madison Square Garden for God's sake! Then suddenly, without warning, like a thief in the night, it all comes to a screeching halt. Why? Because of a 4 letter word that has ended more wrestling careers than steroids, painkillers, and alcohol combined:

HEAT

What is "heat"? That's a great question. The dictionary has one definition. But that's not the kind of "heat" I'm talking about. Behind the veil, the wrestling world is a delicate place. Heat means something else there. This type of heat can ruin your career before it even starts. While there is no definition found in the mainstream dictionaries for this phenomena, it can be defined as such:

HEAT: A black cloud that follows an individual after a personal conflict or misunderstanding between two or more individuals backstage.

When you contract a bad case of heat, you may find yourself disliked or outcast for something you did or didn't do, whether accidental or otherwise. You may not even ever find out what it was that you did. Sometimes heat is genuine and makes sense. More often than not, it is based on jealousy, or a simple misunderstanding. Let me put this in layman's terms: sometimes someone is just straight hating. One could liken it to having a bad case of the cooties. In fact, that's a great way to put it: heat is cooties revisited- for grown-ass, mature, adult wrestlers.

In this memoir you will get a front seat experience on a number of times I got heat. For instance, I'll regale you with such stories as

* The time I was scolded backstage after my debut match on TV by a WWE legend, icon, and Hall of Famer

* The time I was personally punished by the face of the company

and of course

* The "Tweets Heard 'round the World" that landed me in the hot seat in Connecticut

…plus many other nerve-wracking experiences!

In most instances in my career I would rather have contracted the Ebola virus than have gotten heat. (From what I've read, the survival rate of Ebola is slightly better.)
   In some extreme cases (as in, you have heat with someone higher on the totem pole than you, i.e. a "Top Guy") the similarities to Ebola increase, as you will find yourself socially quarantined. No one will eat with you in catering, no one will ride with you to the next show, and essentially no one backstage wants to be caught speaking with you or having any type of association with you whatsoever.
   Also, much like having Ebola, once it is diagnosed, it is then reported to the center for disease control i.e.- the Top Guys on the roster and/or "The Office." Heaven forbid the heat is with one of them! In that case, you're basically screwed. The is no cure in sight. There are three ways this can play out:

1. You can try to stay under the radar, accept some sort of punishment and let things cool down

2. Your career can die a slow, miserable death

3. You can be spared the torment and euthanized quickly and easily. You'll get released, or "Future Endeavored," as they say, within a week.

   I have seen superstars with so much promise, charisma, talent- the whole package, watch their career's go up in flames faster than a gasoline-soaked paper bag in hell, due to this insidious epidemic.
   The following is a real life example of a situation that I witnessed firsthand. (By the way, I'm earning myself more heat this very second just by writing this...)

MR BIG SHOT

My first month "on the road" (as in, touring with the WWE main roster), I witness a coworker get some serious heat for doing something that, honestly, I didn't personally see anything wrong with. The man in question had been on the road a few months before me. On this particular day, we both pulled up to the arena at the same time. He was dressed nicely (as any professional ought to be), with a jacket, polished shoes, and sunglasses. He looked like what he is: a Superstar. (We are WWE Superstars, right?) So here's how he contracted the HEAT...

When we got our bags and walked into the arena, he went around and shook everyone's hand, as we are supposed to. (God forbid you miss one person's hand. The slightest slip-up in the handshaking ritual of wrestling- neglecting the hand of just the right person- can earn you nuclear levels of heat. But, I digress.) As my peer approached one particular main event talent, in order to shake his hand, I noticed the veteran's facial expression quickly change. With a look of disgust, he proceeded to call the rookie out and embarrass him. "Who does this kid think he is? Big shot, huh? Shades in the building?" Needless to say, the rookie removed his glasses immediately, and smiled, nervously. He tried to explain himself. He stated that his hands were full and he was going to remove them as soon as he got to the locker room. The top guy didn't care to hear his explanation. That poor guy walked around on egg shells for the rest of the day. With the exception of him speaking in his television segment, I didn't hear him utter one single word for the duration of the show! Because one veteran didn't like the fact that he wore his sunglasses indoors, this guy now had heat in the locker room, and was scared of his own shadow.

Now that I think about it, as I look back at my career, I'm surprised that I made it eight years. The start of my career was similar to the end of it, in that I felt like I was a walking furnace. In other words, I had major heat. As a matter of fact, before I even signed on the dotted line I got major heat with my trainer and the owner of the developmental school I was attending. That could've ended my career and sent me packing with a one-way Greyhound ticket back to Penn Station.

Throughout my career, I've been subjected to countless instances of heat. Some might say I've had more experience with heat than Lebron James. Some heat was severe, and some was less so- just kinda like little sparks. There were definitely times that I deserved it. Hey, I was 21 when I signed my contract, mistakes were bound to be made. Other times, I got heat that was completely ridiculous and unfounded. To be honest, the majority of the time I was the victim of heat by association. Speaking of that heat by association...

At this moment I would like to acknowledge and to give a special shout out to Shad Gaspard! I love you bro.

OHIO VALLEY WRESTLING

Unlike other sports and athletic ventures, the road to becoming a professional wrestler isn't as cut and dry. With basketball, football, baseball, or hockey, even, there is usually a very clear path one follows. Your hope, as an athlete, is that you will be scouted by a college with a strong athletic program, that you will play well enough within that college to be drafted into the league, you will then compete in your sport on a professional level, and so on and so forth. You get my drift.

Now, when it comes to making it into the "big leagues" in the wrestling world, it's a lot different. When I was coming up, there were really only two "schools" you could attend to get noticed and eventually- if you were lucky- be signed by the WWE. One of the major schools was Deep South Wrestling, or DSW, which was located in Atlanta. The other was Ohio Valley Wrestling, which is better known as OVW, in Louisville, Kentucky. DSW is now defunct. OVW, on the other hand, is still running strong, training wrestling hopefuls and putting on shows all over the great state of Kentucky, USA, every single day of the week.

I eventually decided that my childhood dream was going to become a reality. Not that I wasn't ever sure, it was just time to make it happen. By the age of 18 I was serious enough about wrestling that I moved to Louisville and start learning the tools of the trade, and so, I proudly think of OVW as my alma mater. The lessons I learned in OVW are invaluable, even to this day. I came in contact with so many colorful characters. I interacted with people from varying walks of life. Wrestling at OVW was really my introduction into adulthood. I was forced to get a good understanding of how the world works, and, more importantly, how to be professional. I also learned first hand how to avoid, deal with, and handle... *heat.*

My first week after moving to Louisville, I formed a big brother/little brother relationship with wrestler Elijah Burke. Elijah had been living in Louisville and training at OVW for a couple of months before my arrival, so I took him under my wing (just kidding- it was the other way around). He quickly brought me up to speed and taught me the ropes. I remember one particular conversation where he was advising me on the *Do's and Do Not's* of the wrestling world there at OVW. He advised me that there was definitely a hierarchy at OVW, and that since I was the new kid on the block I was undoubtedly at the bottom of it.

Some of the customary practices that I was expected to adhere to were

* **To be sure to greet and shake everyone's hand when entering the building**

* **Always maintain humility**

* **To help build the wrestling ring and take it down at the end of OVW live events**

And if you were ever awarded the privilege of wrestling at a Live event, you better

* **Not complain if you get hurt (Hurt, Not Injured)**

* **Not leave during the show. You were expected to stay the entire time.**

I was told by Elijah and others to these things, play by the rules, and that I just might be alright. If I failed to do them, especially as a new guy, the inevitable result was...*heat.*

Let's say for instance you were at the show and someone higher in the totem pole saw you earlier. Then you mysteriously disappeared at the end of the show, aka, you left early. You my friend, have heat. Please understand while there is an aspect of the wrestling world that is based on brotherhood, it is also *very* dog-eat-dog. It is a business that is built on bloodthirsty competition, to say the least. I have witnessed wrestlers throw other wrestlers under the bus, well, just because. For example, I remember several times when a wrestler slipped out of the arena early, unnoticed by the higher-ups. He's free and clear, right? Wrong. Another wrestler who also saw the individual leave might casually ask out loud, "Has anyone seen so and so?" That is a classic manner in which wrestlers use passive aggressive techniques to tattle on each other. Yeah. The hating is real. It is very real. And guess what? That guy who was tattled on? He's now guilty of leaving early, and he now has...*heat.*

DO YOU KNOW HOW TO FU*@ING READ?

There is one particular situation that really stands out in my mind from my days at OVW. Although the entirety of my time there was very memorable, there is one particular circumstance that I remember as the first time a fire was really lit up under my ass. Before I teamed up with Shad and became one half of the wildly popular WWE tag-team known as Cryme Tyme, I was part of another duo. My very first tag team in OVW was called "The Gang-Stars." My partner's name was Durty. Durty would later be known to the wrestling world as Abraham Washington, and later as AW. Durty and I were invited to an important meeting regarding OVW's TV show by the Head Trainer, Al Snow. Usually, the only people allowed in that particular type of meeting are developmental wrestlers that are already under contract. Our third time going to the TV meeting, there was a sign on the door which read

"IF YOU ARE NOT IN THE CONTRACT CLASS, YOU ARE NOT TO ATTEND THE TV MEETING AT 12PM!"

For some reason, I thought that sign did not apply to Durty and I. I mean, shit, at the time our tag team was hotter than fish grease mixed with hot sauce, and besides, Al Snow invited us. Surely that sign didn't apply to the Gang Stars, right?
WRONG! Not only did it apply to us, it was specifically written *for* us!
So, we went to the meeting. The whole time, I was smiling inside, thinking "I'm special. We're the only students in the amateur class invited to this meeting. When the meeting ended, as I was walking out of the door, I heard a thunderous voice from above yell out "JTG, WHAT THE FUCK ARE YOU DOING HERE? CAN YOU FUCKING READ?!"
My first thought was, "Is that you God?"
Then, I heard the voice again- "I said, *can you fucking read!*"
I was in a state of pure, utter shock. Was I supposed to answer? Or was it a rhetorical question? Wide-eyed, like a deer in headlights, I responded in a very low tone, "Yes." I looked up and I see the owner and founder of OVW. Clearly, he was PISSED.
"THEN WHY THE FUCK ARE YOU HERE?"
I just stood there. What was I to do? My own father never spoke to me like that. I

was not mentally prepared for this. I wasn't ready. After we looked in each others eyes, for an uncomfortably long time, he finally spoke again.
"GET THE FUCK OUT!"
Guess what I did? Like a real "G", I reached down deep into my inner thug and did what any BK cat would do in my position. I got the fuck out! #NOTSOTHUGLIFE #GOCRYINTHECAR

The Gang-Starz. We were bad azz.

HIRED...

It was the absolute best day of my life! As I was working at the daycare at Gold's Gym in Louisville, Kentucky, I got the world-shifting call I worked my ass off for. I trained and worked and sacrificed for four years there at OVW, and finally, this was it. I got the call as soon as I opened up the nursery. The phone rang and the head of WWE Talent Relations was on the other end. He said "How you doing kid. Vince really likes the work you've been doing down there at OVW. How would you like a job?" I thought of my five year-old self jumping off my mother's couch. This was the moment I had been working for my whole life. No more garbage $100 pay checks! No more clearance rack steak! Goodbye used 1992 Saturn! *I'm about to be rich, bitch!*

...AND ALMOST FIRED

My first time being called up to the road was exciting and nerve wracking at the same time. Shad and I were told to drive to RAW from Louisville that Monday morning, and the little time I spent at home, I spent getting myself together for my first day on the job. One of my close friends, Haz, whom the wrestling world knows as "Armando Alejandro Estrada" ("Ha-ha!") helped me prepare for my first WWE TV. Haz treated me like a younger brother, and in typical older brother fashion, he let me borrow some clothes. I took a suit, shoes, and some button down shirts from him, because at the time I didn't own any of my own business casual clothes. (Give me a break- up until a week ago, I worked at a gym daycare!) By Sunday night I was pretty much ready to go but there was one thing missing. This one thing was important- it was a key aspect of my appearance. That one thing? *I didn't have my hair braided.* There was no way I was going to walk up into that arena with my hair looking like who-did-that-and-why? So I called my hair braider and made a late night appointment, because that evening OVW had a live event. And, of course, Shad and I were required to be there. A few moments later I received a call from Shad.

SHAD: Hey Jay, who's braiding your hair?

ME: Crystal. Why?

SHAD: Can she do mines too?

ME: She's doing mines late at night, Shad.

SHAD: She doesn't have to do it late tonight. She can do it this afternoon.

ME: We can't do it this afternoon. We have a OVW show to go to. You know that.

SHAD: No, we're all good. I spoke with Al. We have to be at RAW on Monday. That's a priority. That comes first.

Something in my gut felt uneasy about it, but I decided to move forward with Shad's plan anyway. I mean, why would he lie? We both had too much to lose at that point. (Right?)

While Crystal braided Shad's hair that afternoon, I heard my phone go off. It was a text message from, guess who? You got it: none other than OVW Head Trainer Al Snow.

The text read: "Where are you?"

At that moment, anxiety hit me hard like Ike Turner. I felt my chest tighten. I showed Shad the text. He looked at me as if he were bewildered and confused. He said, "Just call him. We're good."

So, I decided to man-up and call Al. Before I could even get out "Hi" he said "Where are you?"

ME: Ughhh, I'm getting my hair braided with Shad. Shad told me that...

He cuts me off.

AL SNOW: Getting your hair braided with Shad!!!

ME: Shad said-

Cuts me off again.

AL SNOW: YOU GUYS HAVE A MATCH!

ME: Shad said-

Again.

AL SNOW: STOP RIGHT THERE! Do you have my number?

Me: Yes.

AL SNOW: There should be a button on there that lets you magically contact people that you want to communicate with.

Me: ...

AL SNOW: This is unacceptable.

ME: Sorry, Al.

AL SNOW: Oh, you and Beavis are going to be sorry, alright! I'm going to have to write you guys up.

ME: I understand.

AL SNOW: I hope you guys hair looks *very* **nice and pretty. That's going to be the most expensive hair-do you ever had!**

  A couple of days past and we started to feel good about the situation again. We went to both Monday Night RAW and then Smackdown on Tuesday. It felt like all was forgotten.
  We finished that loop by driving back to Kentucky on Wednesday morning. On the shuttle ride from the rental car agency, my phone rang. It was the head of Talent Relations, the same person that called just a few days prior to offer me my contract. But this time his voice was much less than jubilant.
  "So, what is this I hear about you guys missing a house show down at OVW?"
  "Sorry, sir, It was a misunderstanding. We were getting ready for Raw on Monday and Shad said-"
  He cut me off. I was getting used to that.
  "You guys were getting your hair braided. I should fire the two of you! If it wasn't for the money that we already invested in you guys, I would be handing you guys your pink slip. I'm very disappointed in the two of you. Especially you, JTG. You worked too hard to get called up, for you to do something so stupid and jeopardize it all. I'm going to have to fine you guys $1000.00 a piece."
  As I listened to this, I felt my blood start to boil. All the while, I was staring a hole into the side of Shad's big head. Shad just sat there, staring at me, and asked, "What did he say? What did he say?" I hung up the phone.
  "You owe me $500.00, Shad."
  Shad, If your reading this- I want my money! I'd prefer all crisp, large bills. And try to make sure they're all facing the same way.

10 MATCHES IN ROW

Shad and I had been on the road for a little over a month. We were trying to keep our noses clean and stay under the radar after our last run in with the law. But it that seemed somehow, despite my greatest efforts, *heat* followed us.

On our way home from both RAW and Smackdown, during a brief layover in Atlanta, Shad checked his voicemail. There, awaiting both of us, was a message from Talent Relations. I had to admit, at first I thought we were being *Punk'd*, or that we were the butt of some sort of mean, cruel joke. But this was real. Very real.

The message instructed us to report to OVW as soon as we landed. Apparently, due to the fact that they suddenly realized that Vince had never seen us wrestle (I know, right?), we were now being required to go to OVW morning practice...that same morning. And not just to train. That would have been too easy. We had to wrestle- and film- not two, not four, not even six matches. How many, you ask? TEN. In a row. Yes, ten matches in a row. Wtf!!!

How did we find ourselves in this predicament? Let's rewind this story back to two days prior.

In true Shad Gaspard fashion, during a TV run-through at Smackdown, Shad was standing around talking to one of the developmental guys from DSW. Apparently the DSW talent told Shad that he was required to return to DSW practice immediate upon returning from TV loop. Shad apparently found it necessary to brag that we, as OVW guys, had the luxury of going straight home from the road in order to sleep and recuperate. As I'm sure you've already guessed, that got back to the office, and then guess what followed that. Yup: *heat*.

HEAT 101
If one of your co-workers is voices a complaint to you about something, don't aggregate the situation by telling them how good you've got it.

Not only did this braggadocios statement come back to bite *him* in the ass, it bit the shit out of me too.

I was livid. I was physically and mentally exhausted from traveling. I had my mind set on having a nasty threesome with my pillow, and comforter. But instead of going home, resting, recuperating and having sweet, sweet dreams, I now had to drink a pack of Red Bulls and go live out the absolute nightmare of ten matches in a row.

Shad, if you reading this, make that $500 + 8.99 (for the Red Bulls).

THE HEART BREAKER

Since signing my contract in July 2006, I had been working hard juggling the WWE road schedule and the OVW training schedule. I was about to be rewarded. Somehow, after all the previous shenanigans and run-ins with the office and our good pal *heat*, Shad and I were still employed, and the day I had been waiting my whole life, finally arrived.

On October 16, 2006 **Cryme Tyme made their television debut on Monday Night RAW.** I was so HYPED! I was *all the way* turned up! If the dial only went to 10, I was at 1,000. I wasn't nervous, either. I had too much adrenaline rushing through my body to be nervous. If you watch the video of our debut, you'll see that I was so energetic and bouncing around so much that my hat flew off of my head and one of my chains broke.

After we won our match against the Spirit Squad, we did a classic backstage segment with King Booker and Charmell. It was really one of the best days of my life. We had an amazing debut, the crowd loved us, our co-workers congratulated us- I was on cloud nine. I thought there was nothing that could ruin that moment. Until...

There was one particular Hall of Famer that wasn't particularly happy with my entrance. A few weeks prior to our TV debut, Shad and I were working a non-televised live event. After our match, this particular Legend pulled me aside. He spoke to me in a very calm tone, and he warned me that my hand gestures were very similar to his own tag team's signature hand gesture. According to him, my hands almost crossed each other in the general vicinity of my crotch. Like a good rookie, I apologized, assured him that it was an accident, and promised that it would never happen again.

Many wrestling fans would be shocked to find out how over-protective some of their favorite wrestlers are when it comes to their signature moves, ring gear, catchphrases, and yes, even hand gestures. After all, these are the ingredients that make one Superstar stand out from another, and really, that's how we make a living and pay the bills.

Although I apologized to this Legend, I was certain that the movements I used in my entrance were so wild and all over the place that no one could possibly ever mistake them for his signature hand gesture. But, since I knew he was watching me closely, I made sure from that point forward to not to cross my hands anywhere near my crotch AT ALL.

However, there was another live event where he accused me of doing it again! Now I was paranoid. I didn't know what to do. My entrance was a key part of JTG's persona. I didn't want to be creatively limited and overly self-conscious of my hand movements. Wrestling in front of millions of people on TV is hard enough. This was an unnecessary distraction.

Now that we established the back story, fast forward to what should have been the best day of my life.

After our backstage segment with Booker T, I decided to watch the rest of the show with a few of the other wrestlers on the monitor in the talent viewing area. Out of nowhere, this Legend (and childhood hero of mine, one who I adored so much, in fact, that I used to dance around the house to his theme song wearing nothing but my Ninja Turtle underwear) was in my face, with his fingers pointed, centimeters away from poking me in the nose, screaming at the top of his lungs!

"Not only did I warn you once, I warned you twice! And the third time, you did it on national TV! You have NO RESPECT for me or this business!!!"

Then he stormed off.

WTF!

After letting that soak in for a few minutes, I came to grips with the fact that the Superstar I had watched and loved since I was four had just scolded me like an ugly step child.

I had to think quick. I did NOT want heat with this guy. I went looking for him, and, guess what I did? Yep. Once again, like a real "G" I reached down, deep down into my inner thug, and did what any BK cat would do in my position. *I apologized my ass off!*

I assured him that he was the last person I would EVER want to piss off, and told him how much of an inspiration he was to me. Needless to say, he wasn't really moved by my speech. He replied, "Just don't let it happen again. I'm tired of you young guys coming up here, thinking you can do whatever they want to do."

To this day I still go back and replay my entrance. I don't think I ever did anything wrong. But I want you readers to do some "cross" examination of the evidence yourselves (pun intended). Watch the footage and holla at me on Twitter @JTG1284.

THE WINDOW SEAT

At 21 years old, I had never been to Europe. So, you can imagine how excited I was to be on my first international tour with WWE. For two weeks I got to tour all over England, Ireland and Scotland. But getting there wasn't as simple as boarding a plane and going for a ride. Just when I thought I was safe, *heat* was lurking just around the corner.

Anyone that has travelled with me knows that I am somewhat of a narcoleptic when it comes to flying. I fall asleep pretty easily on planes. As a matter of fact, it's not only on planes. Pretty much it's whenever I'm traveling anywhere, regardless of the mode of transportation. Planes, trains, automobiles- it doesn't matter. I board my plane, put away my luggage, take my seat, find my sweet spot, then that's all she wrote! I'm out. On this particular flight, my peaceful slumber was quickly interrupted by none other than *heat*.

There I was, all tucked in and comfortable in my window seat, for my 14-hour flight. I was just starting to doze off when I was startled by the most annoying voice on the whole roster. Through crooked, tobacco-stained teeth, the voice pierced through the sounds of the aircraft.

"JTG! DONT YOU SEE MY TAG PARTNER IN A MIDDLE SEAT?? YOU DIDN'T CHECK TO SEE IF ANYONE ELSE NEEDED YOUR SEAT?"

WTF???

In the wrestling subculture, there is an unspoken rule: if you are seated in an exit row or have a first class ticket, you give up your seat for a veteran, should his seat be less ideal than yours. In this case, however, neither this guy (nor his tag partner) were even remotely close to the "veteran" category. In reality, these two just happened to be there a *tad* bit longer than me. Take that, and couple it with the fact that I carried myself very humbly, and you see why they thought they could big dog me.

This is how I wanted to respond to him: "Fuck you and your tag team partner. I don't give two squirts of rat piss about either one of you."

But what I actually did was look at him like I didn't understand anything that was coming out of his mouth. He mouthed off to me again, so I said "He's not going to do any better over here." His tag partner finally interjected in the most sarcastic tone, "It's okay, it's only a 14-hour flight." I glanced over at him and saw that his legs were crammed up against the seat in front of him. However, I had absolutely no remorse. After all, the two of them treated Shad and I like shit. We already had heat with them and, frankly, I had no desire to get on their good side.

THE MULE

After 14 long hours, we finally arrived in Europe. While I did find my window seat accommodations to be quite comfortable, I was ecstatic to be back on solid ground. We touched down in Glasgow, and, unfortunately, the rest of tour was a blur. I had extreme ear pain for the first few hours following the flight, and I figured my body was having a hard time adjusting to being in the air that long. Needless to say, I wasn't in the best mood. All I wanted was to get my bags, get to my room, and go to sleep.

It was finally time to get off the place. I was retrieving my bag from the overhead storage compartment when one of the boys, a guy who had been with the company for nearly two decades and was cool with everyone, approached me. He leaned in close and asked me to do him a "favor." He never made eye contact with me. He just stared straight ahead. In a very low, suspicious tone, he said,

"JTG, I need you to hold this for me." I looked down, and there in his hand he held what appeared to be about an eighth of weed. I thought to myself, *Of all the guys on the roster, why me?!*

How the hell do I get out of this? I tried telling him I wasn't comfortable and was unfamiliar with the procedure. He ignored me, and instead instructed me to stuff the package inside my underwear, under my nuts. Now, why anyone would want to smoke weed that had been under someone's nuts after a 14-hour flight is beyond me, but, I digress.

At this point two other wrestlers began to chime in, applying more pressure to the situation.

"Come on Jay. This is your chance to get over with the boys."

"You can hit it with us later."

"Come on! Don't be that guy!"

I always thought peer pressure was a just myth. But it's real, people. *Hella real!*

Then out of nowhere, like some sort of super hero, one of the veterans, a real English gentleman, swooped in and saved the day. As soon as he saw me in distress, he swiftly came to my rescue.

"Leave the young man alone. You guys brought your own stuff in so you need to figure it out yourselves. This is his first tour and you're already trying to get him into trouble. Leave him out of it."

And just like that, they backed off.

He then pulled me aside and said, "I know you were in a tough position. Those guys were not looking out for your best interest. I hate to see young talent such as yourself being taken advantage of. I couldn't just stand there and say nothing. You'll be out of a job and under the jail, and they'll continue wrestling, acting like nothing ever happened."

I knew he was 100% right. I don't think the immigration officers would've believed the old "I was just holding it for somebody" cliche. My black ass would've been buried under a European prison, then dug up, then fired, then on the first thing back to Brooklyn with a 5 o'clock shadow beard and a hobo stick and handkerchief tied at the end.

BEAUTY SALON

Before the trip, I imagined all of the things I was going to do my first time in Europe. I eagerly anticipated taking in what each city and country had to offer. I was excited to experience the unfamiliar. But I quickly found out that while the locations of overseas tours may be exotic, we move so quickly from country to country that there really isn't any time for sight-seeing. It's definitely not as glamorous as one might imagine it to be.

Whatever little time I did get, I played tourist. Yes, I proudly took trips up and down the European countryside, and the few sights I was able to see were breathtaking. Although these moments were far and few in between, what really amazed me was the deep and pure love for wrestling these Europeans had. I was surprised to see how engaged and interactive the fans were in each country we performed in. It's a known fact in the wrestling world that some of the best RAW crowds are at the shows immediately following Wrestlemania. This is because these live crowds are usually a strong mixture of American and European fans. The European fans are best known for their wild chants, and so the merging of the two cultures creates an energy in the arena that is electrifying and unlike anything else.

Overall, I had a great time in Europe. I wish I could say it was a flawless trip, one in which Shad and I didn't draw any attention to ourselves or attract anymore heat... But that would be far from the truth.

Let me just preface this story by saying that while I didn't see anything wrong in general with what Shad did. There was however, something wrong with his execution. Very wrong. Very, very wrong.

Wrestling every single day can take a toll on braided hairstyles, especially on the road in a foreign country, far, far away from one's usual hairstylist. After wrestling for seven straight days, let's just say that Cryme Tyme's braids weren't exactly looking fresh. And Shad and I loved to look fresh, especially for TV.

Due to our necessity to look fresh, Shad asked one of the runners at TV to find a beautician to come to the arena and braid his hair. With the hectic, nonstop movement from country to country, plus utter unfamiliarity with our surroundings, we simply didn't have access or time to get it done otherwise.

To me, the logic here is obvious. Since a major part of our job requires that we look our absolute best at all times (and certainly while representing the company in a foreign country), I expected some basic level of understanding.

Shad and I, however, received no such understanding. We simply had too much heat. At that time, Shad and I could have saved a family from a burning building and some of the boys would've spun the story and said, "Cryme Tyme was showing off, they're telling everyone they're big heroes now." It was that bad.

After our match, Shad got his hair braided. Now here is where Shad messed up: instead of finding a quiet, discrete place to get it done, he instead chose to have the beautician braid his hair in the middle of a high-traffic hallway where EVERYONE could see him. That pissed off some of the boys and (surprise, surprise) also got us heat with some of the agents. Talent (especially new talent) was expected to watch all of the other matches in order to learn from them. It was infuriating to the agents that instead of doing that, Shad was in the hallway getting his hair done. Several of the boys said things to me like "What is wrong with your partner?" and "Sometimes, you guys just ask for it." I responded to them by saying, "*Guys?* That's plural. I wasn't getting my hair braided."

The next day I was pulled aside by one of our agents. He said, "Look, I know you didn't do anything to get any heat, and you have been showing a lot of improvement in your matches. But you and your tag partner are joined at the hip, and if he does something wrong, the both of you will have to feel the sting."

He then informed me that Cryme Tyme was booked to work the Great Khali in a handicap squash match. A squash match is an extremely one sided match in which one performer dominates the other and quickly defeats him with no difficulty whatsoever.

Ladies and gentlemen, I now introduce to you:

"A SQUASH MATCH"
STARRING: THE GREAT KHALI
(ALSO BRIEFLY FEATURING: CRYME TYME)

Right from the bell, I take Khali's big boot, get up, get chopped on my head by Khali's enormous, giant, heavy hand (which really hurt like a bitch, by the way), and then stay down for the rest of the match. Then Shad (the man of the hour and the reason for the season) attempts to hurt the giant with some offense of his own, quickly fails, and also receives a painful chop. Then Shad takes Khali's finisher ("The Punjabi Plunge") and gets pinned.

That match was booked purely in order to punish us. The *entire show*, in fact, was re-arranged to punish us. Our originally scheduled opponents (the team we were supposed to wrestle before Shad's hair-braiding incident) for that night wound up working a six-man tag that evening. In other words, they had a fun, easy, entertaining match, and we got both our asses pathetically handed to us by a giant. I sometimes can't believe the petty lengths the people in that company will go in order to punish

people.
    On nights like that one, I wished I could pinch myself and wake up from what surely was just a bad dream.
    Nope! This wasn't a dream; this was reality. *Heat* was my reality!

WRESTLER'S COURT

    During one trip overseas, I made a new friend. Well, maybe I'm using the term "friend" loosely! I met a girl, and she was one I wished I had never met, spoke to, or had any private interaction with, because of all the stress and grief she caused me afterward.
    One night after a show in England, I was with the boys at the hotel bar. I noticed that a particular female had her eyes on me. (Can you really blame her?) This woman was so into me, and made it so very obvious that one of my colleagues picked up on it. Now this was not just any co-worker. This was the leader of the locker room, the champ himself. It started to get late, so I threw down my ninja smoke bomb and disappeared (aka, I very discreetly snuck out of the bar and snuck back up to my room). I made my way to my room, undressed, and got comfortable in my bed. The phone rang. I answered it. It was the champ. I thought I was going to get heat for leaving without saying goodnight to everybody, but that was not the case.

CHAMP: "Hey JTG, hope you're not sleeping. I have a beautiful young lady that wants to hang out with you."

ME: "Hey Champ, I'm actually in my bed and I'm exhausted. Are you referring to the English chick in the red top?"

CHAMP: "Yup, she's on her way up to your room. I sent her up a few minutes ago! Don't disappoint me and you're welcome!"

    I was tipsy and exhausted. I laughed to myself. It seemed like I was waiting for a delivery from DomiHOES, Booty-Hut or Little Skeezers (with a side order of peer pressure). A few seconds later, I got a knock on my hotel room door.

ME: "Who is it?"

HER: "Room service!"

      It was 3:00am. I knew damn well it wasn't room service. Still unsure (and still tipsy), I opened the door. There she was, the English chick in the red top with a look of lust. She let herself in and at that very moment JTG was a victim of rape. I was obviously too tired (and too tipsy) to defend myself against her. Yeah, Im more muscular and probably had 60 pounds on her but her will was strong. There is no doubt about it: she took advantage of a young, fresh-faced, wide-eyed, innocent JTG. If you don't believe me I have no problem getting the rape doll and reenacting what she did to me.
      About an hour later, she left my room with a big smile on her face.
      "Thank you for a good time. You take care now, okay handsome?" She shut the door behind her as I laid across the bed, tipsy, exhausted, and victimized.
      And I *was* a victim! That's my story, and I'm sticking to it!
      After a few months of mentally recovering from the scars of this sexual misconduct, that night came back to haunt me. Before my night of debauchery in Europe with the British babe, I had actually met her a few months prior. One of my colleagues introduced her to me as "one of his road chicks." Are you asking what a "road chick" is? It is a polite wrestling term for a groupie.
      On the night she took advantage of me, I didn't even think about her association to my co-worker. It never crossed my mind. (I guess it wasn't on her mind either, judging by the way she performed.) But when my colleague, who I actually considered to be a friend, found out about the situation, he was hurt. I'll never forget that fateful Sunday night when he called me. He sounded like a sad little boy who had lost his dog (no pun intended).

WRESTLING PAL: Hey Jay, what's up? You know [insert groupie name here]?

ME: Yeah, I know her.

WRESTLING PAL: Did you guys-

ME: Yeah, but she raped me!

WRESTLING PAL: I can't believe you, Jay! I told you that was my personal road chick!

Uncomfortable silence.

WRESTLING PAL: Let's just talk tomorrow.

Upon reflection, I thought to myself: *Self, a road chick is a groupie, right? Right.*

I then asked myself a follow-up question: *Then isn't a 'personal groupie' an oxymoron?*

Why yes, Jay, it most certainly is.

I could not understand for the life of me why my wrestling pal was so hurt. If he had such a serious relationship with the British babe, I honestly was not aware of it. And why was he so mad at me, and not her?

When I got to work the next day, for some reason almost the whole locker room knew I had a late night rendezvous with my colleague's "personal road chick." I couldn't believe how fast this news had spread! Sometimes it could be so boring backstage in the locker room that the boys would make a big deal out of nothing just for their own entertainment. The news spread throughout the locker room, and it seemed like the roster was choosing sides. The guys' opinions on the matter were split. Some of them said I was a rat-wrecker, and some disagreed and said, no, that's what groupies are for, and that one guy can't hog up all the groupie love. To make matters even worse, my colleague's close friend was going around telling everyone that I slept with his best friend's girlfriend! That was the version of the story that eventually got to the top executives in the office.

This wasn't something I could be fired over, but it was a direct attack to my character. The chatter went on for weeks and I just wanted it to stop. It got to a point where something had to be done. My colleague decided that he wanted justice, and I, on the other hand, just wanted the nightmare to end. Since we both needed a resolution, he had me summoned to *Wrestlers Court.*

Forget the court shows you see on TV. Wrestlers Court is much worse. In Wrestlers Court, the locker room is the jury, and a top guy is the judge. In our case, The Dead Man himself was set to preside over our case as the Honorable Wrestlers Court Judge. JBL acted as Prosecutor and represented my colleague. The day of the trial (which was to be held before that night's taping of Monday Night RAW), I had to scramble to find an attorney of my own. In addition to securing my wrestler representation, I was also strongly advised to sway the court's decision by buying beer for all the boys. Since things weren't looking good for me, I was also instructed to purchase special liquor for JBL and The Deadman, in order to further help my cause.

Before arriving at the venue, I went to a liquor store and spent over $400 on alcohol. To me, that was well worth the investment. I needed to win. If I lost this case, I was going to be sentenced, and the verdict could have been deathly severe. The punishment would have been something like carrying other wrestler's bags for months, or not being allowed to change in the male locker room for a whole year, which are things that may sound silly to an outside person, but, in reality, greatly inconvenience the life of a wrestler.

That day before RAW, there was a lot going on. There was to be a fake funeral service for Vince (his character had "died" a few weeks earlier), which meant hours and hours of rehearsals for the entire roster. In the midst of preparing for that, I had to find a credible lawyer. I was in a tough spot. Not many (if any) of the boys who I thought were qualified enough to get me out of this mess wanted to defend me.

I finally got a little help from my buddy Armando Estrada. While we were in catering, Armando pointed out to me an ECW Legend, who was sitting nearby reading a newspaper.

Armando said, "Look! He's reading a newspaper. He's got to be smart! Ask him to defend you."

Look. I know that merely being able to read a newspaper in no way makes one qualified enough to be a courtroom attorney. But this wasn't real court, this was Wrestlers Court. I didn't need a real lawyer. I just needed someone who was well-respected by the locker room to speak on my behalf.

I was desperate, so I took Armando's advice. I humbly asked the ECW Legend to represent me in Wrestler's Court. Thankfully, he obliged. He said he was honored to be my attorney, that he had a strong defense, and that he was excited to win the case. Whew.

Throughout the day I saw my wrestling pal a few times. As he passed me in the hallways, he said, "You're going down! " That definitely intimated me. I'll be honest; it looked like the jury would most likely favor him. He had been around much longer than me, and was really well-liked among the boys. All day guys kept asking me was I ready."This is big, Jay," they would say. Others antagonized me by saying things like "You should just quit now and get a job at Subway, make it easy on yourself!"

At one point, I even heard the Deadman cynically ask, "Where is this court case taking place again?" This was really happening.

The time was getting closer to my court appearance, which was scheduled to after the final rehearsal. The entire roster and WWE staff was called to sit in the stands around the ring. I shit you not, my whole body went numb and I started sweating like Kim Kardashian at church. Vince was out there, Stephanie, the guys from the production truck who you hardly even see, writers, agents, Michael Hayes- everybody you could possibly think of. They were all ringside.

I knew this story had become big in the locker room, but I didn't think the whole company would be taking part. As the crowd got thicker and everyone was finding their seat, the boys were looking at me like, "Oh, shit, you're in trouble now, JTG!" Even my courtroom opponent looked shocked.

Finally, just when I thought we were about to begin, things took a different turn. Something strange happened. One of the top guys in the company dropped to his knees and began to cry. I didn't know what to think. But I did know that he clearly wasn't crying *for me* like that. I was very confused.

A few moments later, Vince entered the ring and informed everyone that Chris Benoit and his family had been found murdered in their home.

It was a shocking moment. Instantly, I had mixed emotions. Clearly, I was deeply sad that someone I respected and idolized as a child growing up was murdered. Certainly, I wish a less tragic incident could have disrupted my case. Of course. Something like that should never happen, and it was mind-blowing and painful that it happened to someone we were so close to and worked so closely with. However, if I were to say that I didn't feel some tiny, little bit of relief that Wrestlers Court wasn't happening...well, I would be lying.

When we left ringside, most of the boys were more shocked than anything. I guess for me, having already dealt with the emotions of preparing for my trial, it hadn't really sank in yet. When I finally got back to the locker room, I was told by several guys how lucky I was that the trial was postponed. That postponement ended up being an indefinite one, because that edition of Wrestlers Court never ever happened.

The day my trial was slated to happen, both the RAW and the Smackdown rosters were all together as one locker room, because of the TV funeral that was to be held for Vince. That gathering of the entire roster was the perfect setting for Wrestlers Court. It was months before we were all scheduled to be together again, and by the time it could happen, the excitement over me and the British road chick would long since have faded.

Me and my buddy are cool now, and has he helped me a lot through the course of my career. I'm glad we didn't let a rapist, aka the British rat, get between us.

The moral of this story is...well, Chris Brown said it best: "These hoes ain't loyal!"

THE DAY CRYME STOPPED

It was a Sunday in September of 2007. My bags were all packed and Shad and I were headed off to "The Motherland" Africa for a WWE tour. Only a handful of talent get to go on the international tours, and we were picked. I couldn't have been more excited. Before we began the Africa tour we had a few pit stops to make: a live event in Indiana, and a RAW taping in Ohio, both of which we were scheduled to work Lance Cade and Trevor Murdock. To be quite honest, I didn't like them, and the feeling was definitely mutual. They made it very clear that they didn't like Shad and I, and they made both our lives very difficult. They threw us under the bus every chance they got, and made it hard for us to work with them in the ring.

On that Sunday in Indiana, tension between us was at an all-time high. Cade and Murdock made it obvious that they were frustrated that they had to work us for a week straight. While in the locker room they found every way to make it hard to put our match together.

They shot down every single idea we had, no matter what.

"What if- "

"Nope, we're not doing that."

"How about we- "

"That doesn't make any sense."

"Okay, well, what if we- "

"That's stupid."

(Getting the point?)

After trying extensively to work with them, Shad just said, "You know what, whatever happens out there, happens."

We heard our music hit and we just went out there ready to put on a good show, despite the fact that we didn't know all of the details of the match. However, we figured since we knew the finish, and we worked each other often, we could "call it on the fly" out there in the ring.

During a pivotal point in the match, I was knocked to the outside of the ring. I was to play dead on the outside of the ring for a while, then make it back in just in time- just before the referee counted to eight- as we had done countless times before with these opponents. On this particular night, however, Cade and Murdock decided to fuck with us. Unbeknownst to us, they instructed the referee to speed up the count so that I would be disqualified.

When the ref counted me out, I was confused. I knew I rolled back in on the 8 count. *What the hell just happened?*

I laid on the apron and heard Shad yelling to the ref, "I saw that! That's bullshit!" Lance and Trevor were walking up the aisle, laughing, pointing at us, and yelling "Stupid! You two dummies."

Shad was furious. And thanks to Cade and Murdock's hilarious prank, the crowd was not entertained. Instead, they were confused and angry, and a large number of the people were chanting "Bull-shit! Bull-shit!"

From my position on the apron, I watched Shad grab the ref and rough him up. Then he lifted him up onto his shoulders horizontally. He yelled, "Hit our finish! Hit our finish!" So I got up, ran, and we hit the ref with our double team move. After giving the ref our move (the "G9") the crowd went crazy. We brought the excitement back up after that weird count-out finish. To add insult to injury, Shad took the ref's belt off and auctioned it to the crowd. This was Wrestling 101: the babyfaces (in this example, us) are supposed to leave the crowd happy after the match, especially if they are screwed out of a win (in this case, via a fast count-out).

When we returned backstage, all hell broke loose. As soon as we came through the curtain Shad was immediately pulled by an agent into a locker room. I followed behind but was told by the road agent "This has nothing to do with you. I just need to speak with Shad." I'll never know exactly what that agent said to Shad in that impromptu meeting. After Shad got out of the locker room from being scolded, the *heat* got more intense.

We headed to the talent viewing area to finish watching the show. As soon as we sat down the top guy in the company began to berate Shad and to insult his intelligence for making the call to hit the ref with our finisher. Then he insulted us both by saying, "The only reason you guys are so popular is because of two words. I don't even know why you guys are here." He then told Shad that he needed to apologize to Cade and Murdock.

Shad stood up for himself and said "With all due respect, I'm not apologizing to them. What they did out there was not professional. If they have a problem with us we can take care of it in the back. Not in front of a live audience." After that, I believe that Shad earned himself a little respect. But that didn't stop the inferno that was already lit and burning back in the office.

On our way to Ohio for Monday Night Raw, Shad got a call from the Head of Talent Relations. He spoke to him very briefly, then quickly handed me the phone. As he spoke with me, I could tell the tone in his voice was a mixture of anger and disappointment.

"Tell me what happened out there. Why didn't you stop and control Shad? You know better."

I thought to myself, *Control Shad? Shad is a grown-ass, six foot seven man.* I was at a loss for words.

"We're going to have a meeting in the morning. Come see me in my office when you get to the arena."

My immediate thought was "This is going to be one hell of a fine." Nothing could've prepared me for the reality of what would actually go down.

The next day at RAW, we were called into the meeting. As we sat down, I started thinking, *How much this time? Five thousand? Ten thousand? Twenty thousand?*

The meeting opened with the Head of Talent Relations telling us that he was extremely disappointed in us. "I put my neck on the line to get you guys up here. I believed in you two. The crowd loved you two. You both were doing so well. I'm sorry to tell you guys, but I'm gonna have to let you go."

Both of our jaws dropped.

Shad began pleading our case: "What? Your gonna fire us? We don't smoke, drink, or do any drugs, and your gonna fire us for a mistake?"

Then Shad did something that left me in amazement and in shock. He then said, "I understand if you fire me, but don't fire Jay. This had nothing to do with him." I looked at Shad and almost wanted to give him a hug. *Almost.* He finally took responsibility! My Shad was growing up right before my eyes.

Unfortunately, his best efforts were unsuccessful.

"No, you guys are a team. I cant just let one of you go. I'm gonna get Shad a plane ticket back to Texas, and you're gonna have to drive back to Louisville, Jay. It's only three hours away. You can't stay for the show. You have to leave immediately."

He then gave us a hug and said "You two keep your noses clean. The door is always open." We were then escorted out by security. That drive back home to Louisville was the longest, saddest three hours of my life.

COMEBACK

Everything happens for a reason. Looking back on it now, I'm glad we were fired. The time we were away from the company (six months, to be exact) definitely gave us time to mature and appreciate the opportunity that was before us. I was able to do some traveling and personal reflection. Deep down in my gut I had a feeling that we would be back eventually. I did not, however, expect to come back so quickly.

While visiting family in Trinidad, I received a call from Shad stating that we needed to go to Booker T's wrestling school in Houston as soon as I got back to the States. Apparently Shad got a call from someone from the office saying they were interested in potentially bringing us back, so we needed to brush up on our tag team mechanics.

When I got back to Louisville, I was literally home for a few hours before I was off again. Once in Houston, I stayed at Shad's house as we trained at Booker T's. Shad and I worked hard there. We were excited that we might have another shot. We wrestled his students, getting as much practice as we could. It was there that I started to develop my signature move "The Shout Out." The Shout Out was my take on a Japanese move that Shad showed me footage of   After a few weeks, I went back home to Louisville. That's when I got the call from the Head of Talent Relations. They were bringing us back! It was at a lower downside of our original contract, of course...but **THEY WERE BRINGING US BACK!**

The day after Wrestlemania XXIV, we made our re-debut in Orlando, Florida, against none other than- you guessed it- Cade and Murdock.

As you could probably guess those two were not happy to see us back. And to make it sting even more, not only were we back, but they had to lose to us that night on RAW. During the middle of the match, the crowd erupted into an impromptu "Welcome Back!" chant! That was the icing on the cake.

As my mother always says, "Every setback is a set-up for a comeback." And boy was that a comeback!

SHADE ON THE SHADES

As I grew up watching wrestling, I idolized Bret "The Hitman" Hart. I wanted to follow in his footsteps, and to emulate his career. Bret had a customized, cool jacket, so I had to have customize, cool jacket too. Brett Hart had his signature shades, so naturally I wanted my own signature shades as well.

On October 26, 2008, at last it seemed like that dream was finally coming true. I debuted my trademark "Yo, Yo, Yo!" shades in front of millions at the *Cyber Sunday* Pay-Per-View event at the US Airways Arena in Phoenix, AZ. The next step in fulfilling my dream was to get the shades in the hands of the WWE Universe. The demand for the shades was very real.

After showcasing the shades, in true Hitman fashion I took them off and gave them to a fan. Fans in every arena around the globe would ask me where they could get a pair.

Finally, after months of conversations with the lead coordinator of WWE Merchandise, we finally got approval for the shades to go into production. Soon they would be on WWE merch shelves at every arena. (Cue Louie Anderson in *Coming to America:* "And that's when the big bucks start rolling in.")

Before you get all excited for me, curb your enthusiasm for a moment. Let's rewind to a totally unrelated circumstance a few weeks earlier...don't worry, I'm going somewhere with this...

I received a phone call from the WWE magazine and was asked to do an interview about Cryme Tyme. During the interview, the writer asked me to give him a few words to describe my relationship with Shad.

My response was "friendship, bond, loyalty, respect..." and then I caught myself. I quickly asked the interviewer to refrain from putting the words "loyalty" and "respect" in the same sentence. He replied "Okay, I understand. I get it. I know how some of you guys can be sensitive about your gimmicks and catchphrases."

Fast forward back to a few weeks later. That same day I got the green light for my shades... was also the same day I got the red light! The interview was released in

WWE Magazine, and guess what it said. I don't even need to waste time spelling it out, do I?

I was in a bathroom at the TD Bank North Garden Arena in Boston, MA, using the throne. I heard a voice over the stall, "Hey, JTG? Is that you in there? I was reading the latest WWE magazine. Interesting article with you and your tag team partner. Nice choice of words."

I already knew where he was going with this. I immediately started to plead my case. I told him that a lot of the article was embellished, and that I told the writer not to use those two words, especially not in the same sentence.

I finally came out of the stall. He looked me dead in my eyes and said, "You might be telling the truth. The magazine guys are known for putting words in peoples' mouths to make an exciting article. They've done that a few times to me also. But there still has to be consequences and repercussions. This can't go unpunished. You know those cool shades that you have coming out? We're gonna have to put those on hold. That will make us 'Even Steven.'"

Just like that, in the blink of an eye, quicker than a hiccup, it was over. The Lord giveth and the Lord taketh away. To this day those shades are still on hold. Sorry I let you down, Bret.

My first time meeting my idol Bret "The Hitman" Hart. Like a little mark boy I brought him my "My Real Life in the Cartoon World of Wrestling" book for him to sign.

The troops wanted to defend our country in style, Akon wanted a pair, and The President never looked more trustworthy.

FINES, FINES, YEAH, YEAH

By 2008, I had moved past the green "rookie" status and into a pretty decent spot on the roster. Cryme Tyme was a fan favorite, and at that point it seemed like we were everywhere. That fall, we worked a two-week tour in Europe, and unlike our first European experience with Cade and Murdock, this time we had a great time. We worked "The Legacy." Cody Rhodes and Ted DiBiase were guys we worked a few times in the past and had good chemistry with. Despite the fun we were having on that tour, it all came at a cost.

One particular night toward the end of our tour, DiBiase hurt his neck in a match. Unfortunately, with all of the travel, strenuous workouts, and normal wear-and-tear from our line of work, injuries happens a lot. They happen even more if you compound this brutal lifestyle with late night drinking each night. Needless to say, the next night he was still in pain. But, as always, the show must go on. Normal procedure when you're wrestling an injured opponent is to "work around" so you can protect him as much as possible. For instance, you wouldn't body slam a guy who tells you his back is injured.

The following night, despite DiBiase's injury, we were scheduled to wrestle The Legacy again. During the match, DiBiase hurt his neck, yet again. (I can't remember exactly what happened- it may have been a clothesline from Shad?) Right before the finish of the match, DiBiase instructed me to give him a belly-to-back suplex. For those of you who don't know, a belly-to-back suplex is a maneuver in which your head is under your opponent's left armpit as you pick him up, lean back, and drop him all the way down onto his back. The one taking the fall is in control of the bump. When we got backstage after the match, our agents pulled all four of us aside. Immediately, I knew Shad and I were in trouble. Here we go again.

Our agent was irate. He began chastising us for being "dangerous in the ring." He was furious about the suplex. He asked me, "Why would you drop DiBiase on his neck like that?" I stood there dumbfounded, hoping DiBiase would speak up on my behalf. He remained silent. When we got back to RAW the following Monday, guess who was called into the principal's office? If you guessed Cryme Tyme, you are right and you win a prize! (Check page 268 for details.)

When we arrived to the office there was a long line of other scofflaws awaiting punishment as well. They were guilty of such offenses as being late for the tour bus, lewd and drunken behavior, damaging hotel property, and on and on.

When we finally reached the front of the line to face the music, we were accused of being "reckless" and told we "didn't know how to wrestle." The our boss posed a question for Shad and I: "What should I fine you guys for injuring DiBiase?" Of course I low balled him, shouting out, "A thousand dollars!" They both looked at me like I was crazy. He then informed both of us that he had just fined one of the Divas ten thousand dollars for being late and almost missing an international flight back home.

"Let's be reasonable here," he said.

Shad then, um, "countered" by suggesting ten thousand dollars, and I almost fainted. Shad then said "That's ten thousand altogether. Five thousand a piece." Luckily, he agreed to that amount, but also stipulated that we had to return to wrestling school for a week. We were instructed to go down to the WWE's Developmental school in Tampa, *FCW*. To make a long story short, Shad and I, who were arguably the most popular tag-team on the roster at the time, were back doing beginner drills!

On our first day after the first set of drills, we had five tag-team matches, back to back. In retrospect, it seemed like more of a punishment than an actual learning experience. What I did learn was that in this business you can't ever think too highly of yourself because the fall from grace is hard. Really, really hard.

THE B WORD

One afternoon, during a taping of Monday Night RAW, I experienced what I would have to classify as one of the most awkward moments in my entire wrestling career. After arriving at the arena and dropping off our bags in the locker room, Shad and I headed down the hallway to catering. Along the way we ran into the Boss's daughter.

Now, this wasn't a company where you're expected to give respect to "The bosses' kid" just because of who they were. In this case, in the WWE, the Bosses' daughter made it very clear that she demanded respect herself because she rightfully earned it. She aspired to be the boss *herself* and Having married one of the most recognizable wrestlers of my generation, she ensured that she was well on her way to securing her own position in WWE history as a shot caller and one half of professional wrestling's ultimate power couple.

As I passed her in the hall I said, "Good Afternoon, Boss Lady," which was my usual greeting and nickname I came up with that described her. She smiled and kindly and replied, "Good afternoon, JTG." This innocent hallway banter would have been absolutely perfect if my tag team partner had not followed it up with his statement. Now, if you ask me, I think he was jealous that I had a familiar nickname for her, and wanted to *one-up* me. As you will discover, this did not work out favorably for him. True to form, the *heat* Shad earned for himself bit me in the ass as well.

Now, in an attempt to give Shad the benefit of the doubt, I would like to take a poll here. Ladies and gentlemen, what would be the most offensive "B word" that a man could use to refer to a business woman (especially if she were in a position of authority)? No, it's not the "B word" you're probably thinking of.

Give up? The word is "Baby."

What in the world would posses a person to greet his female boss with "Hey, Baby. How you doing?" I will never know. However, on that particular day that's exactly what transpired. Shad Gaspard greeted his BOSS by saying "Hey, Baby. How you doing?" Shad Gaspard, ladies and gentlemen.

Her immediate reaction was priceless. The look on her face was terrifying. If I had to guess as to what she wanted to say, it would be:

"What the fuck did you just call me? Are you fucking crazy? Who the hell do you think you are? Do you know who I am? Did you just call me BABY? I'm your fucking boss!"

But we were in the workplace, and she had to remain professional. So what she really said was:

"What did you just call me? Don't call me baby, Shad. If you talk to the Divas

like that, that's fine. But I'm not one of the Divas, and you can refer to me by my name."

Straight Gangsta with it. Then she shot an awkward look at *me*. To make matters worst, once again, the Champ - the Top Guy - The Face of the WWE - just happened to be walking down that same hallway. So, after he boss lady cut her promo on Shad, the Champ looked at Shad and said "Baby?!"

He shook his head and walked away. I never talked too much about The Baby Incident with Shad. It was kinda like watching your best friend getting knocked out and humiliated at the club. You just help him up, and don't bring it up again. (Unless you're writing a book.)

CHOOSE YOUR WORDS WISLEY

I wish I can say Shad learned from that last experience. I really wish I could, but that's not the case. Another scenario where Shad's filter malfunctioned was in Cleveland, Ohio.

We arrived at the arena for RAW and that particular morning, Shad was making a statement. He was dressed to impress! Shad was wearing a tailor made suit and I have to admit, he cleaned up pretty nicely.

Anyway, Shad was getting a lot of compliments throughout the morning. Knowing Shad, I knew he couldn't wait until Vince, or the Head of Talent Relations, or *anybody* from the office for that matter, to see him. When you dress as sharp as Shad did that day, you make a few rounds around the arena before changing so everyone can see how dashing you look. I've been guilty of that myself a time or two. If I'm wearing a nice outfit, I'd make sure everyone sees it, god dammit!

The moment he'd been waiting for arrived. We bumped into "The Game" himself. "Wow, Shad, you look sharp," said the Cerebral Assassin. What happened next? My boy, my homie, Shad Gaspard completely froze!

Shad now had three options:

a) say "Thank you"

b) return the compliment

c) kiss a li'l ass and make small talk

But no, my partner choose-

Z) tell your higher up "I'm wearing this suit just to impress you. I guess this is what it feels like to sell out."

I stood there screaming on the inside, *Why, why, WHY! What would possess you to say that, Shad?!!*
The look on the Game's face read, "What the fuck?!" Then what always happens next, happened: the awkward look at **ME**.
As we walked down the hall I said to Shad " Why the HELL would you say that !?!
He just looked at me and said " Why you think Ill have heat now ?
Whatever…...Fuck it.

JIM HENSON

After a phenomenal run together (although the tag-team titles seemed to be utterly elusive to us during our entire tenure) the powers that be ultimately decided to break-up Cryme Tyme. Shad and I were then left to go our separate ways as solo wrestlers. While I loved Cryme Tyme, I was also intrigued by the possibility of transitioning into singles success. There were however, some demons I would have to face that were left over from my Cryme Tyme days.

One of my first goals of being a solo WWE Superstar was separating myself from the Cryme Tyme image. I wanted a new look, and most importantly, a new theme song. Let me fill you in on a little secret. A large percentage of a WWE Superstar's success is based on his entrance and theme song. If you have a bad-ass theme song and a cool entrance, you've won half the battle. There have been numerous superstars with horrible gimmicks or who were not the best wrestlers, but they got over just because of their theme music.

I'm not the biggest Gangrel fan, but I remember going crazy when Gangrel's theme music hit. Gangrel arguably had one of the best, if not *the* best, theme song and entrance in WWE history! It has to be at least top ten. Gangrel's music hit, he would rise in a ring of fire, walk down to the ring with such incredible swag, drink blood from a chalice then spray it out of his mouth like HHH (or did HHH get that from him, hmmm, I wonder). Then the bell rang.

I knew that if I wanted guaranteed success, I needed to get a new theme song and fast! Not only did I want to get a new theme song, I wanted to be in the studio while it was being produced (just to make sure that when my music hits I was coming out to HOT FIRE!)

During the day at a RAW taping in Chicago, I knocked on Vince McMahon's door to speak to him about getting JTG a new theme song. I explained to Vince that I wanted a new song to help launch my solo career that would also separate me from my Cryme Tyme days. I also mentioned that I wanted to head to Connecticut on my off days to help produce the track because I wanted it to match my charisma, my style, and to make sure it was certified HOT FIRE! Not only did Vince say yes, he complimented me for taking initiative in my career. He gave me Jim Johnson's email and phone number to start the process.

Jim Johnson is the man responsible for all the theme music you hear in the WWE today. I was excited at the prospect of working with him. As soon as I got Jim's number I called him. I told him what I wanted, and he told me to send some examples. I was hyped. Send examples, no problem! I had a buddy of mine go in the studio to whip something up for me so he would know exactly what I wanted when I got to the studio (aka that HOT FIRE!).

A week later, after promo class, which was a class taught by Vince himself, I had a conversation with the boss about a new character idea that he loved involving a muppet. During the conversation, he was tossing around names of various employees that I had never heard of. He gave me a list of the names and numbers of people that he wanted me to contact. I called and emailed every single person that he told me to. The following week I followed up with the boss about my progress. He then asked me who I spoke with. For the life of me I could not remember their names. I only remembered their job titles and roles in the company. Vince then gave me a lecture, a "life lesson" if you will, on how important it was for me to remember names. He instructed me to me stay on top of the task at hand and not to forget a name. I was definitely up for the challenge.

The following week, once again, after promo class, I went to follow up with Vince about the muppet idea. I told him about my progress and he seemed pleased. He then asked me how was my theme music coming. I replied "I just emailed Jim Henson. I'm waiting for him to get back to me."

Vince looked at me shocked and said "What did you just call him?" He face read something along the lines of "I just told this motherfucker to learn names a week ago! You called the man behind our music the man behind Kermit the frog? What the fuck?!"

I said, "I meant Jim Johnson. I said Jim Henson because we were just talking about muppets." I tried to laugh it off nervously, but he didn't think it was funny. His face remained stern. *Damn, Why didn't I just call him Jim?* I knew at that moment that I fucked up big time. After that, there was very little interest in my muppet idea. And on top of that, as you can probably recall, "Brooklyn, Brooklyn" is what continued to play when my music hit. There would be no hot fire. There would, as always, be *heat*, though.

JTG, CAN I TALK TO YOU?

As I'm certain that I mentioned before, I was a big Hitman fan growing up. As a kid, I wanted to do everything Brett did. There was a spot Brett did way back in 1990 in Toronto at *Wrestlemania IV*. It was the Hart Foundation versus The Bolsheviks. The spot was so minor, but to me it was always the little things that made a superstar stand out. The spot exuded so much swag, that I said to myself at five years old, "Self, if I ever become a WWE superstar, I'm doing that."

What was the spot, you ask? It was at the very end of the match when Brett pinned Boris Zhukov. The Hart Foundation just hit their finisher "The Hart Attack." As Bret was pinned Boris, he extended his arm out and counted one, two...and on three, he looked at the camera and counted it. Yup ! That's all it was. I wanted to do that.

Well, I kept that promise to that five year old me, and I did do it. But it cost me. I was actually able to hit that spot twice. The first time I was able to pull it off against some locals on RAW.

The second time I wasn't so lucky. That time, it was against an active Superstar on the roster. When I came back from my match I was feeling myself: I hit my Bret Hart three-count spot and I *won*, which rarely happened in my career. As I waited for my opponent to come back to thank him and to make sure he was okay, somebody called my name.

"JTG! Can I talk to you for a minute?"

The person that wanted to speak with me was someone who I highly respected and looked up to in and out of the ring, and by the look on his face he didn't look to happy with me.

Damn. What did I do know.

As I made my way to him, he pulled me out off to the side and said, "Let's talk over here, privately."

I was worried. I did not want heat with this guy. I followed him to a very secluded area.

This must be bad.

"Is everything okay?" I asked.

"Everything is cool. Your match was fine. But it was at the end where you did this three-count thingy and looked at the camera. Save that for locals. People never see them again so it doesn't matter. Don't do that to guys on the roster. That buries them, and they have to come back the following week, so it makes them look bad. That's all I wanted to tell you."

I thanked him for his advice. He was right. Even though Bret did it, it was a different time and circumstance. Additionally, I respected this Superstar ten times more because of his professionalism. He pulled me aside, out of the eye of the rest of the crew, and he didn't make a scene in front of everybody (like other top guys would do).

He could have easily embarrassed me in front of the whole locker room, but instead he displayed true leadership and carried himself like a top notch role model, to be an example to everyone else in the locker room. This superstar is a true stand up guy that genuinely cared about the business and careers of Superstars that he saw potential in.

After that night, even though I loved the Bret Hart three-count spot, it's something I'll never, ever, *EEEEEEEEVER* ...do again.

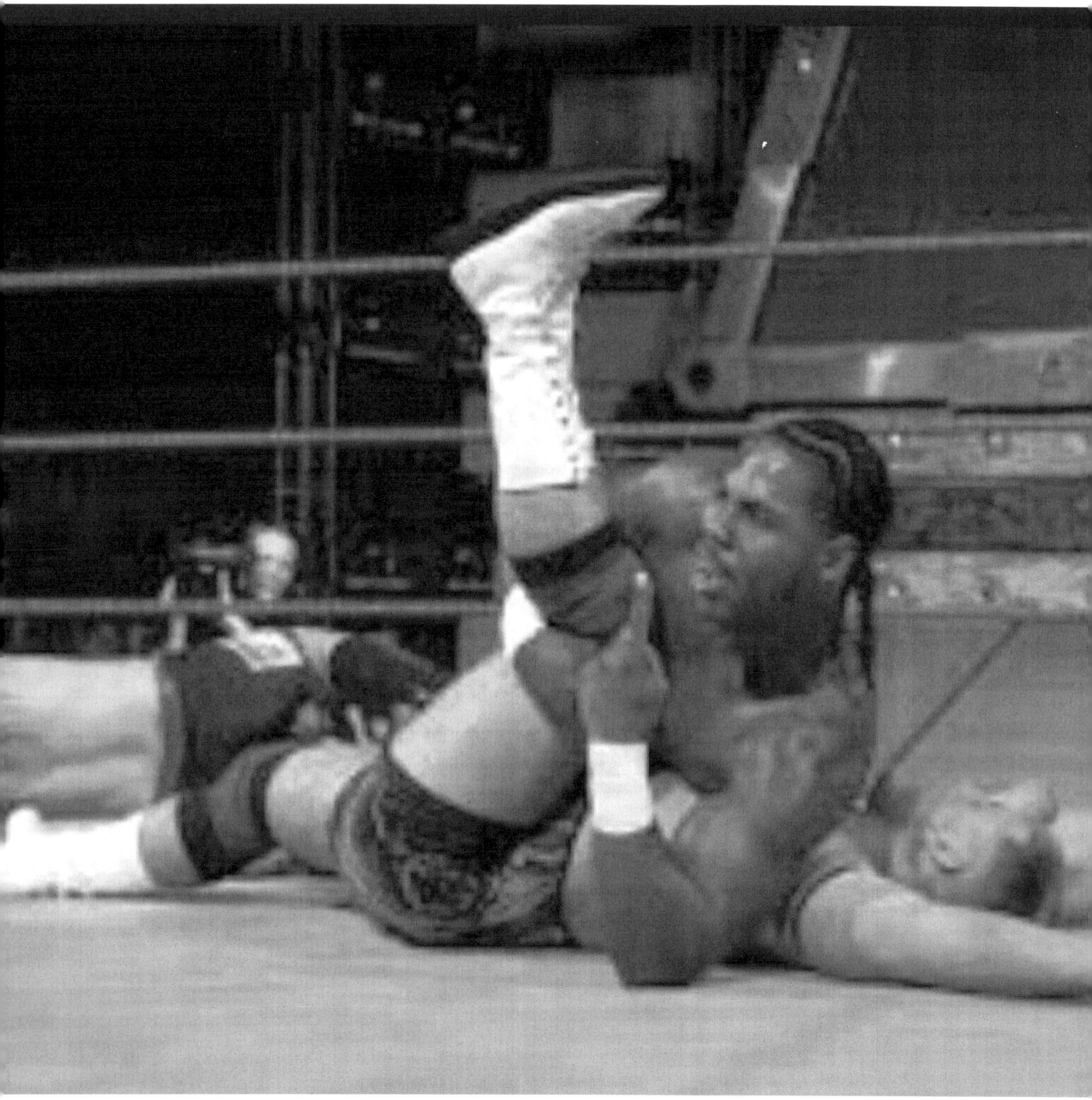

MY FIRST SIGNS

Before I became a WWE Superstar, I made a promise to myself. I said to myself, "Self, no matter what happens in my career as a professional wrestler, don't ever, ever, ever *ever* become a jobber."

What is a jobber? A jobber, or "enhancement talent," is an individual whose sole purpose is to make other talent look good. They hardly get in any offense, they have no story lines, no mic time, no TV time, no theme song- no nothing. Jobbers just magically show up in the ring after a commercial break and get their asses handed to them.

My plan if this was ever to happen to me was to leave the company, plain and simple. I planned to leave, go somewhere else,, make a name for myself, and comeback. JTG was too talented and charismatic to be an enhancement talent. Don't get me wrong, I don't mind losing, and I don't mind making another superstar look good when it's their time to shine. That is business. But when it becomes my sole purpose in life to lose, then it's a problem.

If you followed my career, you're probably asking why I *didn't* leave then? The answer is simple: life happened. I had a family. I had a baby on the way, and I could not make that sacrifice at the time.

The first time I sensed myself going down Jobber Ave, I spoke up immediately. In doing so, I believe I pissed off the wrong people. It was during a Smackdown taping that I found out early I was working one of the company's up-and-coming rising stars. I knew I was losing, but I was excited to work with this individual. I had a lot of respect for what he did in the ring, and I was looking forward to making him look good.

When your putting someone over strong in a match, there is percentage formula agents like to use to structure things. In this particular match, I was told to split it thirty percent in my favor, and seventy percent in his. The point of this particular match was to build his character and strengthen his current storyline.

Now here is the issue. We had all day to plan out a match in which we both came out looking like stars, and we also furthered his character's development. But when it came time to put the match together, my opponent avoided me all day. When I did catch up with him (which was several times through out the day) he brushed me off and said, "Just listen to me out there." That was a red flag.

As we got closer and closer to our match, I still had no idea what we were doing. We had a couple of minutes of TV time, so I definitely wanted to talk it over. Before I knew it the match before us was coming to a close and I still knew nothing. I had enough and I went looking for him.

When I found him I said "what are you going to do to make me look good before you cut me off and beat me?"

His reply was, "This match is all me. You're not getting any offense. Just try to fight back if you can."

I looked at him like he was crazy and said, "I'm going to make you look good but there is no way I'm going out there and just letting you beat me up for five minutes."

He said, "Thats what Vince wants."

I looked at him like he was full of shit. "Vince wants you to squash me?"

"If you don't believe me, ask him."

So I did. I marched up to Gorilla Position, where Vince sits and watches the entire show, and asked him out loud so my opponent could hear me .

"Vince, is this a squash match? Am I suppose to just go out there and get beat up for the entire match and lose? That's what he said," and I pointed at my opponent.

Vince looked at me, baffled, and took his head set off. He said "No, this is not a squash match." He looked at my opponent and told him, "Give him a shine spot, cut him off, and hit your finisher."

My opponent looked pissed. He rolled his eyes and said, "Alright, whatever."

I'm not calling my opponent a liar. But if he was telling the truth, I made Vince change his mind quick because I wasn't having it!

When the bell rang, we pretty much had a shitty match. The lack of communication that it takes to have a good match was very noticeable to the trained eye. Both of us did a great job *not* selling each others punches and kicks. He didn't care to do good business, and so I didn't care to make him look good. When I took his finish, I didn't sell it like I would have sold it. I just kinda *reacted* to it.

I guess he didn't like that. So, out of nowhere, and with no warning, he puts on his second finisher, a submission move.

I think to myself, *Woooooord! This mothafucka tryin' to play me, huh? Okay, let's play.* In order for him to win I had to tap out. Guess what I did? I stayed in that submission hold nice and long, until it was really uncomfortable and awkward. He literally yelled at me out loud twice to tap out. It was so awkward WWE had to edit it and switch the camera shots around to shave of a few seconds.

When we got to the back, all hell broke loose. My opponent decided to yell at me in front of the rest of the boys, and I gave in. We had a huge shouting match in front of everyone. I'll take some responsibility and say I was wrong for feeding into the shouting match.

In retrospect, what I should have done was say, "You're upset? Let's go deal with this somewhere else, privately, like men. Take that however you want to take it." Anyhow, he wound up apologizing to me because the whole situation was handled unprofessionally. We shook hands and killed whatever tension we had.

To this day, he and I are civil. We are not the best of friends, but we are cool, so to speak, but we do have mutual respect for each other. Looking back on that night, I might have earned some respect from my peers for standing up for myself. But I definitely got some heat from the agents, supervisors, and office who now viewed me as difficult to work with.

For all the up and coming talent in the business who sees their skills being wasted, I recommend you follow your gut. Say what's on your mind and do what's best for your brand. Know your worth. As long as you're respectful, you won't look back on your career and have any "I wish I did that instead" moments.

THE MASSAGE

During my time with the WWE, the company contracted massage therapists to be backstage during live events. Although it was paid for by WWE, and was definitely a necessary service for our line of work, the majority of the talent didn't taken advantage of it.

So, one day during one of our talent meetings at Raw, the Head of Talent Relations brought up the fact that the talent wasn't utilizing the service, and if we didn't start to use it they would discontinue providing it. Now you would think that grown men that get hit with chairs, thrown into tables, and slammed consecutively night after night would be *running* at the chance to get a free massage! It makes absolutely no logical sense that a massage therapist would sit in a room backstage, twiddling his thumbs. But that's exactly what was happening.

There was like an unspoken stigma attached to someone getting a massage. Everyone (and when I say "everyone" I'm referring to the mid-card guys, because the Top Guys didn't give a shit) was afraid that if they were seen getting a massage they would be looked upon as thinking too highly of themselves.

I recall a time when I just started out on the road. It was near the end of a show, and the message therapist saw me attempting to walk by. She damn near begged me to let her work on me. She had been backstage the whole evening and barely anyone had been to see her. After some serious convincing, I reluctantly agreed to the massage. I laid down on her table and she started to work her magic.

Just as it was getting really good, it was like I heard a record scratch and one of the top, TOP guys, and I mean topper than top, stopped dead in his tracks and said, "Hey Shawn! You've got to come see this! One of the OVW guys who hasn't even been on the road for a week is getting a massage." I leapt off of that table so quick, I must've broke some sort of Guinness World Record. The massage therapist started to laugh. Looking back, if you ask me, I think it was a setup. But it didn't matter: the damage was done. I was scarred for life.

But after that talent meeting, I decided to live life on the edge and take advantage of the all expense paid massages. Although my career was in purgatory at the time, I was still scheduled to travel weekly. And with most of our shows being on the east coast and my home being on the west coast, the travel schedule alone took a toll on my lower back.

The following RAW, I decided to cash in my "Massage in the Bank" Briefcase. Out of respect to the guys who were on the show, or who worked the live events that weekend, I decided to go when I knew everyone else would be too busy to get a massage: during the first half of the show.

I got to the (mostly) abandoned room, and she started to work on me. I dozed off about midway into the massage when I was startled awake. I heard a knock, the sound of the door open, and then the sound of the door slammed shut.

I lifted my head and asked her "Who was that?"

She replied "I don't know. Some big guy."

Thanks a lot lady. That did absolutely nothing to help me identify the door slamming culprit. Anyhow, after feeling revitalized and refreshed, I returned to the locker room where one of my comrades informed me that a particular superstar came in and said, "Why is JTG getting a massage? He's not even on the fucking show!" and then proceeded to talk shit about me. When I found out who it was, I was very disappointed. I was especially let down because this guy had been on the roster for so many years and was somebody that I thought I had a good relationship with. I guess I just expected more from him.

I mean, all he had to do was say "Hey Jay, do you mind if I jump in here real quick? I'm on in a few." I would have gladly gotten up off of the table and gave him my spot. But instead, he decided to throw me under the bus.

My colleague told me, "Jay, not only was he trying to get you heat- he went out of his way *just* to do it! He was walking by, saw a crowd of us in the locker room, sat down, interrupted the conversation that we were having, talked shit about you, then left shortly after."

This particular superstar didn't even regularly change in the main talent locker room. He changed in an entirely different locker room. This meant that his sole purpose in stopping by was *just* to get me heat! What kind of shit is that? I was appalled.

However, I decided that I wasn't going to allow his antics to affect me. If he wanted to act like a big, overgrown child, that was his problem. It did not mean that I had to join him. I decided to go on about my business and not to even address his locker room tantrum.

So the following week, guess what? I went to see the massage therapist again. Now, I was still considerate of the talent that was preforming that night, so again, I opted to go at a time that I knew wouldn't be busy.

When I got to the massage room, it was so deserted I swore I saw a tumbleweed roll under her table. I asked her, "How many people have you worked on today?" She replied "About three or four. I've been trying to pull people in as they walk by, but no one was interested."

I said, "Well, if anyone comes to the door wearing tights, let me know. Because they're probably preforming tonight. I'm just here because my lower back is killing me and your not busy." "Don't worry, she assured me. I haven't seen anyone in the last couple of hours." That was all I needed to hear.

I took off my shirt and laid on the table, and with such impeccable timing that it was borderline creepy, the same Superstar from the previous week barged in. Without making any eye contact, he uttered "Jay, I need this room." It was like he was trying to big dog me and assert his authority.

I politely got up off of the table and gave him my spot, all the while thinking to myself, "That was some bitch shit he just pulled."

If by any chance that particular superstar is reading this (you know who you are) and have a problem with this chapter, come see me. I'm not hard to find. I can't beat you but I will gladly slap you, have you chase me, and when your big ass gets tired and you're gasping for air, I'll whip your ass while your trying to catch your breath. Ha, ha, ha. Just serious.

THE TWEETS HEARD 'ROUND THE WORLD

I worked for biggest company in sports entertainment, traveled the world, and was on network television regularly. That definitely looks and sounds amazing from the outside looking in. But the reality is it has its disadvantages, too. Don't get me wrong, I'm grateful that I was afforded the opportunity to showcase a craft that I was very passionate about, on a global scale. However, when my passion and love for the business is twisted and used against me, then we have a problem on our hands. As much as I loved wrestling, I'm no one's fool.

In June 2013, the roster received what was *supposed* to be two big pay days. When the vast majority of the talent received their checks, they couldn't believe what they saw. The check we received was both an international payout and a WrestleMania payout combined together. The international portion of the check included shows we ran in Brazil, while the Wrestlemania portion covered the entire Wrestlemania week's events. Even if you weren't on the card for the main event, Mania week is all "hands on deck" and the whole roster participates in the festivities. We were all was under the assumption that it would be overall a pretty nice looking check. However, we assumed wrong.

When we got our checks that Monday, the entire roster (well maybe not all of the entire roster but it's safe to say most of the roster) was sent into an uproar. For some ungodly reason, unbeknownst to any of us, our payday was *exactly the same cost* as our work visa. In other words, we made a profit of zero dollars for that entire tour.

Many of us mid- and lower-card talent thought at first that we were the only ones being screwed, but we soon found out that was not the case (this time). Oddly enough, this phenomenon wasn't isolated just to the talent that was lower on the card. This injustice was across the board! Upper mid-card guys got played, too! We all felt the cold, clammy slap from our corporate pimps. The realization sank in: we traveled for hours and hours and hours, and put our bodies on the line on foreign soil...all for free! This was absolutely ridiculous. And it was only the beginning. If the Brazil check was a pimp slap, then our WrestleMania check was a cold, hard, backhand.

During WrestleMania, talent is encouraged to bring their immediate family and loved ones for the week to enjoy all the WrestleMania festivities. It's like a week-long, very expensive, company picnic. Although WWE does take care of the hotel accommodations, there is the cost of airfare for your family, rental car fees, hotel parking, and food to pay for all week long. In other words, all of the expenses associated with a family vacation. Then, if your attending the Hall of Fame Ceremony, there's the cost associated with the required attire for the event, which is very formal. And believe you me, those are just the basics. I'm not even going to get into the more detailed charges. But, you get the idea. WrestleMania week is very expensive for the talent. Having said all that and giving you an overall overview of what we incur financially up front for this event, when you receive your WrestleMania check a couple of months later, as a business person you want to make a profit. Unfortunately, in this scenario, not only did a majority of the talent who was not on the WrestleMania card fail to break even, it actually cost them more money to be there.

Needless to say, we were livid when we got our checks. We were also insulted that the company combined the two paydays we'd been waiting so long for. It was almost as if they wanted to make the check appear larger than it was. I tell you, they truly have mastered the art of illusion.

That morning, all of the talent was lined up by the door to speak to the Head of Talent Relations, who (surprise, surprise) was very dismissive. So instead of talking to the middleman, I decided to chat with The Game himself.

The entire day I tried to speak with the Cerebral Assassin, and that entire day he avoided me like a cold sore. On three different occasions I walked up to him and asked him for three minutes of his time.

The first time was in the hallway in the morning. He said,
"Yeah, as soon as I finish talking to Vince we can chat." He stepped into Vince's office. I must have waited for about ten minutes when he began to make his way out of the office. He sees me, but it appears he "forgot" something so, he proceeds to turn back around and goes right back into the office. I stood there and continued to wait for

another ten minutes, and he never comes back out.

After waiting for another forty minutes, one the agents (who I didn't even see walk in the office) stepped out. He saw me and said, "You've been waiting here for over thirty minutes. Are you waiting to speak with Vince? I said, "No, I'm waiting for H to come out." He then informed me that The Game was not in there. So, apparently, either The Game has the power of teleportation, or it might just be that he snuck out a back door in order to avoid me. I'm sure he would deny the latter.

I finally caught up with The Game near the ring, where I asked him to speak with him briefly, yet again. "Yeah," he replied "catch me during rehearsals."

I was persistent and adamant about speaking with him, so again, I found him during rehearsals. Then, during rehearsals he said "I'm a little busy- catch me after rehearsal."

After rehearsal ended, he was finishing a conversation with someone, but then looked over and saw me standing waiting, and continued his conversation for another five minutes.

As soon as he stopped talking I interjected and said, "Hey H, I just need to speak with you for three minutes."

Now this is the part where I really felt disrespected.

He said, "Hey Jay, I'm really busy. Are you at Smackdown tomorrow?"

"No," I replied.

"Okay. Let's talk next week then."

He went right back into his conversation, which was mostly him shooting the shit and chuckling with one of the agents. Must have been a *real important* conversation.

I felt low. Lower than the dirt under an ant's belly. I wasn't even worth three minutes? I wasn't even worth him *pretending* like he was busy? The fact is, he didn't want to listen to what I had to say there.

But I was going to make sure he heard me.

That evening during RAW I posted some Tweets in reference to how the company mistreated their talent. I knew going into it that there would be some consequences and repercussions. But at that point, to be quite honest, I didn't really give a shit. I didn't appreciate the mistreatment, the disrespect to me as a man, and the plain, old disregard for myself and the rest of the talent. We were treated like two-dollar whores. Enough was enough. Someone had to speak up. Someone had to get their attention. Someone had to be willing to risk it all and take one for the team. I guess that someone was me.

I *tried* to go the "professional" route. I *tried* to bring my grievances to the boss directly. That didn't work. But I knew in the day and age of social networking, I had the power to be heard not only by the boss, but also by the entire world.

Shit needed to change. As far as working for the biggest company in the world and being labeled "Superstars"- we definitely weren't treated that way. After a show, which entails a physically rigorous day of rehearsing and performing until usually 10 or 11 p.m., talent should not have to cram in a car and drive themselves an average of four to six hours while the stage crew (the camera man, lighting guy and sound guy) take luxury buses with beds. YES- the stage crew and the writers have their own buses!

Our first year on the road after coming from a show, Shad and I almost died because I was so exhausted that I started to fall asleep at the wheel. I lost control of the car, broke through the median and wound up in the middle of two highways. I literally totaled the car. But we must have had angels watching over us because we managed to make it out without a scratch on our bodies. It doesn't take a neuroscientist to tell you that traveling late after performing physically and mentally exhausting feats is very dangerous. However, because it has been accepted as the "norm" amongst wrestlers, it has, and will continue to be *the way things are done.*

I was ignored and blatantly disrespected by my boss the entire day. During the first half of RAW, while I sat in the talent viewing area, I posted my first Tweet.

"The camels back just broke! I had enough of this."

Minutes later, I posted the second tweet:

"As a pro athlete, I'm tired of me and my locker room brothers being taken advantage of. Fans have no idea what we go through. #itsanillusion"

Then the third and final tweet:

"Nobody wants to speak up. Everybody's afraid of losing their jobs or getting taken off TV."

I sat right there with my phone in my hand facing Gorilla position. A few moments later I see The Game's assistant scurrying out of Gorilla with a paranoid look on his face. He locks eyes with me and makes his way towards me.
"JTG, is your Twitter account hacked?"
"No," I replied. "It's working pretty fine."
"Sooooooo, that was you posting those Tweets? Do you want to be here or are you trying to get fired?"
I then proceeded to inform him that I was unhappy, as was a vast majority of the talent in the locker room. He then asked me "Then why did you go on Twitter? Why didn't you try to handle this professionally?"
I then explained to him that I did go that route, but I found that "The Game was playing games." I concluded by telling him, "So let's see where we go from here."
He then looked at me and said, "I don't think this was a smart move."
It wasn't too long after that I was also pulled aside by the Head of Talent Relations for questioning. Then after RAW ended guess who was *finally* available to speak with me? You guessed it! The Game. As a matter of fact, not only did we speak, he also set up a meeting with me at his office in the WWE headquarters in Stamford, Connecticut that Thursday. That Wednesday I was flown to Connecticut and put up in a hotel not to far from the headquarters.
Going into this meeting I knew that there were only a few possible outcomes. I could either get released from my contract, be coerced into asking for my own release of my contract (which would forfeit he ninety days of pay I would be entitled to if the company released me, and would of been very stupid on my part) or I could walk out of that motha with a new contract and get my locker room brothers their just due.

Our meeting was scheduled for 11 in the morning, however, going into it I knew that I wasn't going to see him at 11. This is a heads up to all up and coming talent in the biz: when your boss sets up a time to meet with you and makes you wait for a long period of time, nine times out of ten, it is definitely done on purpose. It is an old psychological trick bosses like to use to throw you off mentally so they can have the upper hand in the meeting. Always, remember to remain patient and stay collected. Do not (I repeat: DO NOT) loose your cool.

I arrived at the headquarters at 10:30, early, and in my business attire. When I was finally called into the office to meet with the game it was 3 p.m. He made me wait for four hours.

I walked into the office and there were two other individuals with him. One was his assistant, and the other was a woman who also handled Talent Relations. This was also something I already anticipated. Honestly, I expected more suits at the meeting, but I guess he thought three would be just enough to intimidate me without being *too* overwhelming.

The meeting went on for a little over an hour. I don't have to spell out to you what happened in that meeting, but let's just say some of the boys in the locker room had their paychecks adjusted, and I remained on the roster for a few more years. *Meeting adjourned!*

THE HEADPHONES

I didn't know it at the time, but it Wrestlemania 29 ended up being my last Wrestlemania with the company. How appropriate then, that it was held in New York, my home state. Backstage there were all types of celebrities, with musicians, artists, and athletes among them. Wrestlemania usually draws that type of crowd, and the fact that it was in New York made it even more accessible to celebrities. There were also representatives from different companies promoting their brands and products. One such company was Beats by Dre.

Throughout the day I noticed numerous colleagues of mines walking around with brand new unopened boxes of Beats Headphones. I, for one, did not own a pair of Beats by Dre and was very tired of getting teased by my buddy Kofi for my Korean knockoff headphones that he referred to as "Heats by Jay." So that day I went on a mission.

I sought out the Beats rep. There was no way that free Beats headphones were going to be given out and I wasn't going to get a pair. That was not going to happen!

When I finally tracked the Beats rep down, he was a very cool guy. He informed me that he had run out of headphones that day but would be at RAW the next day with another limited amount. He told me to look for him then.

The following day at RAW, I didn't see him, and I started to loose hope. Then my buddy Ezekiel walked into the room with brand new headphones and told me on the low, "Your boy is here. He's down by the loading dock and he only has a few more left." I gave Zeke a quick hug for informing me, and sprinted out of the locker room very quickly.

I got to the loading dock and there he was. I gave him some dap (a cool high five) and told him thank you very much. I finally had my own Beats by Dre.

At that moment I felt like a kid on Christmas morning. As I walked back to the locker room I had the biggest most awkward smile on my face. My smile was so obvious that a particular Superstar I walked past asked me, "What the hell are you smiling for?" He looked down and noticed that I was holding a brand new box of Beats by Dre. He then said, "What you doing with those? You got that from the Beats guy? Where is he? I didn't get a pair. You should give those to someone who is more over." Then he walked away.

His words roundhouse kicked the shit out my confidence. My self esteem went from a hundred to zero real quick. I didn't even want the headphones anymore. What I wanted to do was to check his big ass. But, instead, I had to bite my tongue and play politics because of his position and pull in the company. So pretty much, I took one on the chin and walked around feeling like shit for the rest of the day. But that was only the beginning.

Later on, while hanging out by the talent viewing area watching RAW, I overheard two Divas chatting. One of them intentionally started to speak louder so I could hear her, and she said, "I tried to get a pair of Beats today, but someone took three for themselves." Then she looked directly at me and said "JTG."

I looked at her like she was crazy. "Three Headphones!" Not one, not two... but THREE? I said, "Who told you that I took three headphones? That is a hot lie straight from the lips of Lucifer himself!"

She looked at me with disbelief and skepticism, "Like *really*, JTG? You didn't take three?"

"No," I responded. "I only took one pair. Where did you hear that from?"

"I'm not going to tell you. But it was from a reliable source." Then the other Diva chimed in "Yeah, he was walking around telling everyone that you took the last three. Everyone is kinda pissed at you, Jay." I couldn't believe what I was hearing. Why would somebody intentionally lie on me like that and *maliciously* try to get me heat? (I did a pretty good job of getting heat on my own. I didn't need any help.)

After doing some digging, I found out exactly who was running around assassinating my character. It was the same hating ass "Superstar" that destroyed my confidence earlier that day. He was on a roll; two for two.

But here's the thing- this guy is RICH and has a big name. He could just have his assistant make a call to Beats and they probably would have sent him an entire crate of headphones in all different colors. I'll tell you why he was complaining and whining (and he wasn't the only one either). There was another top guy that was also in the locker room boohooing about headphones. Yes, another rich motherfucker, who already had a pair of Beats wrapped around his neck while he was complaining about not getting more free headphones. Let me break it down for you guys- some Superstars have no identity outside of wrestling and feel empowered by their status in the company. They feel that since they have years invested in the company and they are considered to be "Top Guys," (in the locker room, not on TV) that everyone should kiss their ass. They have a superiority complex and get off on treating anyone lower then them on the card like shit. I once overheard that same guy say, "The guys lower on the totem pole need to wait until the top guys are taken care of first before they go running to go get free headphones. Once we're taken care of then they can take whatever is left over. That's how it used to be."

(That type of mentality is exactly why there will never be a WWE union. Because in order to create one you would need the "Top Guys" to agree and stand in solidarity with the rest of the roster. But that would create *equality*, and hence the "Top Guys" would lose their perceived status. But, I digress...)

I went throughout the rest of that RAW receiving a lot of "side eyes" from the locker room. And of course, once again, I never addressed the individual that flat out tried to assassinate my character like Mufasa. In this business, you have to choose your battles wisely, and that was one I choose to leave alone because addressing it would have made matters worse.

MY LAST MATCH

In September 2013, unbeknownst to me at the time, I wrestled what would turn out to be my final match. It was against the infamous Santino Marella. Now, I've wrestled Santino many times before, and every time we faced each other- without fail- I met my uncompromising end his deadly finishing maneuver "The Cobra." As you may know, The Cobra is a ridiculously comical finisher. Therefore, every time I took it, I did my best to "sell it" in as entertaining a fashion as humanly possible. I might have taken the Cobra three different times on television, and each time I tried to outdo my last sell. However, in retrospect, it could have very well been my overly zealous desire to "one up" myself that got me sent home after that final Cobra. Ultimately, I'll never know if that is really what happened or if it was just conveniently "coincidental." However, what I do know is that it definitely got me a lot of heat with the agents backstage, and immediately after that I was home for almost a year until the powers that be eventually decided to release me.

If you haven't seen this epic moment in wrestling history, I strongly suggest, actually, I *insist* that you go on YouTube right now and watch it.

As a matter of fact, even if you *have* already seen it, go on YouTube anyway and watch it again.

I'm serious. Stop reading. Go on YouTube. Type in "JTG SELLS COBRA" and watch it. Now. DO IT!

Okay, phenomenal. Your back! GREAT! Wasn't it bad ass? Although I didn't win the match, once I came back through those curtains, **I felt like a winner**. My peers gave me a standing ovation when I got backstage. Everyone in the talent viewing area got to their feet, clapped, told me how entertaining our match was, and how I made it all complete with the Cobra sell. Now, unless you've had your head buried under a rock, or you're just slow on your uptake, then you must know from reading the previous chapters of this book how hard it is to get even the slightest compliment- let alone a standing ovation- from the boys. This is especially true for guys like like Tyson Kidd. Tyson is a five-star performer, and a tough critic, when I saw him stand up, clapping, and walking towards me saying "Best sell ever, good shit, JTG, "I was proud of myself. I was floating on cloud nine. Until my agent found me.

My agent informed me that while my match was very entertaining, a few of the other agents were pissed about how I sold The Cobra. I asked him what he thought. He told me, "I thought the sell was great! The boys popped big at the monitor, but they're not the ones you need to impress."

That evening at RAW, I had a few agents say things to me like "What the hell was that?" and "What are you doing out there?" A couple of the agents just looked at me, shook their heads, and walked away. Confusing, Huh? To this day, I can't say that I understand it either.

So here is a word of advice to all the future Superstars reading this book:

DO YOU!

When you're out there in that ring, listen to that crowd and react to them. Don't try to please everyone in the back. It is impossible (especially in that business) to please everyone.

I have absolutely no regrets. I can honestly look back and say that I went out there with the cards that I was dealt, and played the shit out of my hand. Not every perceivable loss is really a loss at all. When I wrestle, I perform to be remembered. In my matches, when I'm cutting a promo, even in interviews, I say and do little things that will make JTG stand out. I take my strengths and I magnify them. I am charismatic and I've got a shit load of personality when I'm in that ring, and can't nobody take that away from me.

I will always remember my last match with WWE because, in a way, it kind of mirrored my entire career with the company. I didn't always win, but my performance made you respect and remember me.

THE FINISHER

My eight years with the WWE was bittersweet. As in any phase in life, there are ups and downs; highs and lows. My time with WWE was a fulfillment of a childhood dream. Each thing that I set out to accomplish within the span of my career, I did. Well, actually, there are three exceptions:

1. I never got the opportunity to wrestle in Japan and get my Ribera jacket.

2. I never won a title.

3. I never performed at WrestleMania.

However, I accomplished some amazing, incredible feats. I performed in the very same arena I watched wrestling at as a child, Madison Square Garden, in front of my biggest fan, my mom. I traveled the world. I had the pleasure of working with some of my childhood heroes. I walked red carpets. I played with my own character in video games. I had several of my very own action figures. I was on a first name basis with Vince McMahon!

There are also a few things that I've accomplished that I never anticipated in the beginning of my career. I had the distinct honor and privilege of being one of the individuals to wrestle in the very first match EVER at the Barclays center in my beloved Brooklyn, New York. And I definitely didn't know back in my OVW days that I would make history as the youngest African American to be active on the RAW roster. Who would have ever anticipated, that Shad and I would be classified as one of the hottest tag teams of this decade! I can say with all certainly... not me!

It has definitely been a wild ride. I have more memories at 30 than some people triple my age. I am grateful for every experience, even the ones in the category of *Heat*. Each and every circumstance has shaped me into the man that I am today: a bad-ass mothafucker who don't take shit from no one, a family man, and a boss that's about that *money, money, yeah, yeah.*

Q & A

Q: How do I become a pro wrestler, and what should I expect ?

A: To become a pro wrestler you must give and sacrifice a large portion of your life. You must be passionate about the business, and not in it just for the fame and fortune, because, believe me, you will be highly disappointed. Find a good school (I recommend OVW) and devote all your attention to your dream of becoming a pro wrestler. Everything else aside from that is either a distraction or not a priority. Your training and your workouts come first. Relationships, friends, and family will all have to take a backseat to wrestling. Hopefully your true friends and significant others will stick by you and understand. Last but not least, you must learn to love the taste of shit... and ask for more! In the wrestling business they don't have time for the weak. Only the strong will make it (unless your daddy was a wrestler and he put a good word in for you).

Q: What is your favorite city to perform in ?

A: New York City. I love performing in Madison Square Garden. That's where my Mom took me every month as a child to see WWF live. The whole experience was great. We took the train from Parkside Avenue where I grew up, got off at 34st, and right before we entered the arena we would buy a bunch of tacos across the street from MSG and sneak them in inside her purse. Performing there gave me flashbacks of my childhood. When my music hits, I know I'll get a loud hometown welcome.

Q: Worst city to perform in?
A: Boston. Just kidding. My wife is actually from there, as is my *arch frienemy* Kofi.

Q: What is your career highlight?
A: Although I wrestled countless matches in my career, the one that meant most to me was our tag-team title match at *Summerslam*: **Cryme Tyme vs. The Big Show and Chris Jericho**. Having a match on that card, against superstars of that magnitude, presented Shad and I in a whole new light. It was always a pleasure working with and learning from Jericho. He's truly one of the best in the business.

Because I'm such a mark I personally requested Jericho to put me in the old school "Lion Tamer."

Q: Best wrestler to work with ?
A: I just answered that, you assclown!

Q: Favorite late night snack?
A: My wife. #GIGGITTY

Q: How did your arms get so big ?
A: Tens of thousands of hours with the Shake Weight. Just kidding- go check out my arm routines at *Bodyspartan.com*

Q: JTG, what should I expect from you in the future?
A: If everything goes to according to plan, NOTHING. Hopefully writing stories about wrestling will make me rich, since wrestling itself did not.

Q: JTG, will Cryme Tyme ever comeback to WWE?
A: Never say never. (But probably **never** after this book comes out.)

THE HEAT COMMANDMENTS

Thou shall shaketh the hand of everyone backstage. *Unless you're over.*

If thou art sitting, thou shall stand up to shake someone's hand (especially top guys). *Unless you're over.*

Whilst in catering, thou shall ask everyone at your table if they need anything (drinks, napkins, forks, food) before you get up and leave the table to go get something for yourself. *Unless you're over.*

Thou shalt not walketh into catering with thine shirt off. *Unless you're over.*

Thou shalt not wear shades in the building. *Unless you're over.*

Thou shalt not stand up for yourself if a top guy disrespects you. Although it is advisable to do so as a man....in some circumstances you may have to choose between thine job or thine manhood.

Thou shalt not spread out thine luggage all over the locker room, because other wrestlers need space to place their bags, too. *Unless you're over.*

If you have a bad match, thou shalt not blame thine opponent and try to clear thine name. *Unless you're over.*

If your opponent gets hurt during your match, thou shall make certain to inquire as to the status of their condition constantly. Although it may not be your fault, thou shalt never make mention of this fact. Thou shalt not go try to clear thy name by speaking the truth. The truth shalt NOT set thee free. *Unless you're over.*

Thou shalt not be an *ask-hole*: do not ask questions you already know the answer to, just so you can strike up a conversation with a top guy. It's annoying and top guys see right through it. They will begin to avoid you.

Furthermore, thou shalt not ask a top guy for advice then subsequently fail to apply it. That is major heat. *Unless you're over.*

Thou shall giveth up thine airline seat for a top guy or a veteran if your seat is more accommodating than theirs. *Unless you're over.*

For rookies...thou shall remember names immediately! Especially top guys!

Thou shalt not take it personally when a top guy ribs you. Laugh it off. Telling on them will only hurt you.

Thou shalt not laugh too hard when two top guys are roasting each other. The attention could easily be diverted to you with one simple question: "What the fuck is so funny?"

Thou shalt not complain about being hurt.

Thou shalt not use other wrestlers' signature moves or catchphrases. *Unless you're over.*

Thou shalt not shitteth in other wrestlers' travel bags. *Unless you're over.*

Thou shalt not shitteth in another wrestler's sandwich and watch him eateth it. *Unless you're over.*

Thou shalt never call out sick! Crawl out of bed and catch your flight.

Thou shalt not fucketh another wrestler's wife or girlfriend. *Unless you're over.*

Thou shalt not brag about how over you are. (*Unless you're over.*)

WRESTLING SLANG FOR DUMMIES

Agents
　　Retired wrestlers with years of experience and knowledge who are hired to help current wrestlers put matches together to tell a compelling story in the ring.

The Boys
　　A term used by wrestlers in reference to the males in the locker room.

Bump
　　To fall and hit the mat or ground.
In my humble opinion, bumping needs to be regulated, like in Hollywood. Actors are protected because they have SAG, which is a union.

Call it on the fly
　　A term used by wrestlers to indicate that they will not pre-plan a match, opting to instead let their actions happen organically according to the crowd and natural pacing of the match. Calling it on the fly requires wrestlers to think fast on their feet.
　　With a unpredictable crowd like Philadelphia, it is best to call a match on the fly. One minute a wrestler is a bad guy and then all of a sudden the crowd starts cheering for him.

Cut-Off
　　A term used by wrestlers to describe the part of the match in which one wrestler stops the momentum of the other.
　　"I thought the babyface was just about to win, but just when everything was looking good, he got cut-off."

DSW
　　Deep South Wrestling. A former wrestling school in Atlanta, Georgia. DSW was shut down in down in April of 2007.

Developmental and Developmental Wrestlers
　　Wrestlers who are being groomed to be called up to the main roster to become WWE Superstars.
　　I was in developmental for 3 years before I got called up.

Downside

A downside is the guaranteed minimum a talent can get paid in a year.

Even though I wasn't booked for almost twelve months, I was still receiving my downside.

Finish, finisher, finishing move

A signature move performed by a wrestlers that usually signifies the end for their opponent.

When was the last time I hit my finisher? No, really: I can't remember. Tweet me @JTG1284 and tell me.

FCW

Florida Championship Wrestling. A WWE Developmental Training School that was located in Tampa, Florida, until July of 2013.

Gorilla

The staging area just behind the curtains where talent makes their entrance.

When I'm in Gorilla, I like to do a few push-ups, go over my match in my head, and fantasize about wrestlers having a union.

G9

Cryme Tyme's signature tag-team finishing move. It is a Samoan Drop and a neck-breaker executed at the same time.

Cryme Tyme hit the G9 on the referee, and we lost our jobs the next day.

Heat

A black cloud that follows a individual after a personal conflict or misunderstanding between two or more individuals backstage.

This book will get me a lot of heat, but fuck it.

Jobber

A jobber is enhancement talent. This guy's sole purpose is to make other Superstars look good. Jobbers hardly get any offense, they have no story lines, no mic time, and definitely no meaningful TV time.

Loop

This is a term used by wrestlers to describe a a series of shows traveled back to back.

I remember one week I wrestled an entire loop with a fever of over 100 degrees, but I was too scared to mention anything because wrestlers don't have a union, and we can face serious punishment for complaining or admitting we are hurt or sick.

Mark

A diehard wrestling fan who is not associated with the business. He or she knows that wrestling is somewhat choreographed and that the characters are fictional, but suspends their disbelief anyway.

Marks will wait for hours at an airport or a hotel or restaurant just to see a

Superstar who sometimes they don't even care for.

The Office
The office is a term used by wrestlers to describe the group of individuals back at the headquarters in Stamford who pull the strings.
The office will probably not be happy with this section of the book.

On the Road
A term wrestlers use when they are traveling from show to show.
I miss the fans, but I don't miss being on the road. The travel schedule is brutal.

Over
A wrestler who is considered very popular or well-liked.
Cryme Tyme was over with the crowds, but not backstage.

OVW
Ohio Valley Wrestling. OVW is one of the best wrestling schools in the country. It is located in Louisville, Kentucky.

Rat, Ring Rat, Road chick
A female groupie.
Road chicks sometimes drive and let wrestlers stay at their homes while they are on the road, because wrestlers don't want to pay for hotels and car rentals. Those things add up and cut into their profits.

Rat-Wrecker
A wrestler who takes a rat off the market by getting into a serious relationship with her.

Shine
When a wrestler is looking good at a certain point of a match. This usually comes near the beginning of the match.
I like to get my personality over in my shine. Some wrestlers like to "get all their shit in" and do everything on their moves list during this portion of the match.

The Shout Out
JTG's signature finishing move.
Seriously, I don't remember the last time I hit this on TV. (Somebody look it up

and tell me. @JTG1284)

Squash match - A lop sided match in which one wrestler destroys his opponent and gives him little to no offense.
    A Squash match is a great punishment used to put wrestlers on the roster back in their place for speaking their mind or mentioning the word "union."

Top Guys
    Wrestlers who are the main draw and face of the company.
    In my opinion, guys like Ziggler, Kofi, Alex Riley, and Tyson Kidd should be top guys because of their passion, talent, and work ethic.

Under Contract
    Talent who is signed to a deal and is now considered property of the WWE.
I was under contract with WWE on and off for 8 years.

Union
    An organized group of workers who collectively use their strength to have a voice in their workplace. Through a union, workers have a right to impact wages, work hours, benefits, workplace health and safety, job training and other work-related issues. Without a union, employers have almost all the rights.
    If WWE Superstars had a union, wrestlers could collectively meet and negotiate with management over any issues that effects them without them getting any heat or

some sort of ridiculous punishment for speaking their mind.

Veteran
A wrestler who has years of experience and knowledge. He is usually older and provides guidance to the next generation of wrestlers.
Chris Jericho is by far one of best veterans to work with and learn from in the business.

Wrestlers Court
A court trial held by wrestlers in the locker room that the boys use to sort out disagreements amongst themselves.
If all the boys can get together for Wrestlers Court, I know they can get together to form a union.

WWE
World Wrestling Entertainment, the largest sports entertainment company in the world.

WWE Superstar
An employee... wait, my bad... an **independent contractor,** who works as a wrestler...wait, my bad again... a **sports entertainer** on the WWE roster.
WWE Superstars need to form a union.

WWE Universe
A term used to reference WWE fans worldwide and in other galaxies.

ACKNOWLEDGEMENTS

First off, I would like to give a big thank you to Vince McMahon and the WWE family for giving a young, motivated (yet slightly naive) 21 year-old kid from Brooklyn a shot. Every experience, whether bad or good has helped to shape me into the man I am today. I am ever appreciative.

Next, I would like to thank my brilliant, incredibly smart, talented, beautiful, sexy, mouth-watering, scrum-diddly-umptious wife, Thomika, for lending her writing talent and co-authoring this book. Thank you for being my partner in this project, and also my partner in life. Thank you for supporting me and encouraging me to put these stories on paper and to share them with the world that day I was on my way to pick you up from rehearsal. Thank you, my Hampton Girl, for infusing all of your scholarly, colorful words, in order to help these stories come to life. I love you and our princess, Madyson, more than you could ever know.

I also want to give a big thanks to Rip Rogers and Danny Davis for training me and teaching me the basic fundamentals of the wrestling business. I got large portion of my in-ring confidence from you, Rip. You believed in me from the the beginning and told me that I was a star.

Shad, Shad, Shad, oh, *Shad*. Where do I start? This book could have never been written without you. Literally. In all honesty, I should have just named the book *Shad's Fault*. Ha, ha, ha, just serious. We've seen and done so much together. Thanks for being my big brother for the last decade. Through all of the hell you put us through, you also put us in great positions to catapult our careers. Love you Bro. #PAUSE

I would like to thank my mother, Carol Paul, whose love for wrestling sparked my own. Thank you Mom, for always supporting me, encouraging me and instilling in me that I could do ANYTHING! Thank you for being the catalyst that started it all. Literally. I love you.

I also want to give a shout out to my best friend of over twenty years, Jason Babb @Hovaboss. You were the first person to read my book in its entirety and give me your constructive criticism.

Last, but not least, I want to thank wrestling fans across the globe that have supported both my singles career and Cryme Tyme. I'll give an especially big shout out to my # 1 fan, Flyisha @alisha225.

Thank you to Jason Saint for the pictures back from my OVW days.
Thank you to everyone who purchased this book. I hope that you've enjoyed reading it half as much as I've enjoyed writing it.
CHEA!

Printed in Great Britain
by Amazon.co.uk, Ltd.,
Marston Gate.